Understanding Emotional Problems and their Healthy Alternatives

Rational Emotive Behaviour Therapy (REBT) is an approach to counselling and psychotherapy rooted in the CBT tradition, and one that has a distinctive perspective on emotional problems.

Understanding Emotional Problems and their Healthy Alternatives provides an accurate understanding of the REBT perspective on eight major emotional problems for which help is sought and their healthy alternatives:

- anxiety and concern
- depression and sadness
- shame and disappointment
- guilt and remorse
- unhealthy anger and healthy anger
- hurt and sorrow
- unhealthy jealousy and healthy jealousy
- unhealthy envy and healthy envy.

Rather than discussing treatment methods, Windy Dryden encourages the reader to understand these problems accurately and suggests that doing so will provide a firm foundation for effective treatment. This new edition, updated throughout, reflects the increased interest in helping clients work towards 'healthy negative emotions'.

Understanding Emotional Problems and their Healthy Alternatives will be essential reading for therapists, both in training and in practice.

Windy Dryden, PhD, is Emeritus Professor of Psychotherapeutic Studies at Goldsmiths University of London and is an international authority on Rational Emotive Behaviour Therapy (REBT). He has worked in psychotherapy for over 45 years and is the author and editor of over 250 books.

Understanding Emotional Problems and their Healthy Alternatives

The REBT Perspective

Second edition

Windy Dryden

LONDON AND NEW YORK

Second edition published 2022
by Routledge
2 Park Square, Milton Park, Abingdon, Oxon OX14 4RN

and by Routledge
605 Third Avenue, New York, NY 10158

Routledge is an imprint of the Taylor & Francis Group, an informa business

© 2022 Windy Dryden

The right of Windy Dryden to be identified as author of this work has been asserted by him in accordance with sections 77 and 78 of the Copyright, Designs and Patents Act 1988.

All rights reserved. No part of this book may be reprinted or reproduced or utilised in any form or by any electronic, mechanical, or other means, now known or hereafter invented, including photocopying and recording, or in any information storage or retrieval system, without permission in writing from the publishers.

Trademark notice: Product or corporate names may be trademarks or registered trademarks, and are used only for identification and explanation without intent to infringe.

First edition published by Routledge 2008

British Library Cataloguing-in-Publication Data
A catalogue record for this book is available from the British Library

Library of Congress Cataloging-in-Publication Data
A catalog record has been requested for this book

ISBN: 978-1-032-06707-0 (hbk)
ISBN: 978-1-032-06706-3 (pbk)
ISBN: 978-1-003-20348-3 (ebk)

DOI: 10.4324/9781003203483

Typeset in Times New Roman
by Newgen Publishing UK

Contents

Preface vii

PART 1
Anxiety and concern 1

1 Understanding anxiety 3
2 Understanding concern 21

PART 2
Depression and sadness 37

3 Understanding depression 39
4 Understanding sadness 58

PART 3
Shame and disappointment 71

5 Understanding shame 73
6 Understanding disappointment 89

PART 4
Guilt and remorse 99

7 Understanding guilt 101
8 Understanding remorse 118

PART 5
Unhealthy anger and healthy anger   127

9   Understanding unhealthy anger   129

10 Understanding healthy anger   144

PART 6
Hurt and sorrow   155

11 Understanding hurt   157

12 Understanding sorrow   168

PART 7
Unhealthy jealousy and healthy jealousy   175

13 Understanding unhealthy jealousy   177

14 Understanding healthy jealousy   191

PART 8
Unhealthy envy and healthy envy   199

15 Understanding unhealthy envy   201

16 Understanding healthy envy   212

Appendix: List of eight common unhealthy negative emotions with the equivalent healthy negative emotions, together with their adversity themes, basic attitudes, behaviours and forms of subsequent thinking   219

Index   229

Preface

My purpose in this book is to outline the Rational Emotive Behaviour Therapy (REBT) perspective on the eight major emotional problems that people seek help for and their healthy alternatives: anxiety and concern, depression and sadness, shame and disappointment, guilt and remorse, unhealthy and healthy anger, hurt and sorrow, unhealthy and healthy jealousy and unhealthy and healthy envy. In this book, I refer to the former emotions in each pair as 'unhealthy negative emotions' (UNEs) and the latter emotions in the pair as 'healthy negative emotions' (HNEs). This will be a book on understanding emotional problems and their healthy alternatives, not on how to treat these problems, for effective treatment needs to be based on an accurate understanding of both and this is what I aim to provide here.[1]

While REBT is an approach to counselling and psychotherapy that is rooted firmly in the CBT tradition, it does have a distinctive perspective on emotional problems. As you will see from the following chapters, the REBT perspective argues that:

- People make different inferences in each of the eight UNEs listed above. These same inferences are also present in the alternative HNEs.
- People disturb themselves by holding a set of rigid and extreme attitudes towards these inferences and they undisturb themselves by holding a set of alternative flexible and non-extreme attitudes.[2]
- When people hold rigid and extreme attitudes, they not only experience UNEs; they also act (or feel like acting) in certain dysfunctional ways and think in highly distorted ways. These thinking and behavioural consequences of rigid and extreme

attitudes give expression to these attitudes and tend to reinforce people's conviction in the attitudes.
- When people hold flexible and non-extreme attitudes, they not only experience HNEs; they also act in certain constructive ways and think in realistic and balanced ways. As above, these thinking and behavioural consequences of flexible and non-extreme attitudes give expression to these attitudes and also reinforce people's conviction in these attitudes.
- People can hold rigid/extreme attitudes and flexible/non-extreme attitudes that are specific and general. Their general attitudes influence the inferences that they make in the first instance and then they bring their specific attitudes to create either their emotional problems or healthy alternatives to these problems and the thinking and behaviours that accompany these problems and healthy alternatives. As you will see, the thinking and behaviours that stem from both sets of attitudes referred to above vary according to the emotional problem or healthy alternative under consideration.

The structure of each chapter is quite similar. While this may be repetitive, it will facilitate comparisons across the emotional problems listed and their healthy alternatives and help you to see what is similar and what is different from problem to problem and healthy alternative to healthy alternative.

For ease of reading, I have not included academic or self-help references in the text. Rather, after the chapters discussing the eight UNEs, I have provided a key reference for you to consult according to your specific academic interests as a therapist. I have also provided a key self-help reference for clients.

With respect to gender and the singular/plural issue, I have used the gender neutral plural (they/them/their) when discussing the relevant issues, unless the specific examples indicate otherwise.

Finally, I have included a summary of the material in this book in the Appendix.

Windy Dryden
London and Eastbourne
July 2021

Notes

1 There are many books available that discuss how to use REBT in practice and I refer the reader to these resources. For example, see W. Dryden (2021) *Reason to Change: A Rational Emotive Therapy Workbook, 2nd Edition*. Abingdon: Oxon, Routledge.
2 In this book, I will use the terms 'rigid/extreme attitude' and 'flexible/non-extreme attitude' instead of the terms 'irrational belief' and 'rational belief'. For a full discussion of the reasons why I made these changes to REBT terminology, see W. Dryden (2016) *Attitudes in Rational Emotive Behaviour Therapy: Components, Characteristics and Adversity-Related Consequences*. London: Rationality Publications.

Part 1

Anxiety and concern

Chapter 1
Understanding anxiety

In this chapter, I will make some general observations about anxiety before discussing more specific areas of this disabling emotion. In the following chapter, I will do the same for concern which in REBT is considered to be the healthy alternative to anxiety.

General points about anxiety

In this section, I will discuss:

- The role of threat in anxiety.
- The role of a general anxiety-creating philosophy comprising four general rigid and extreme attitudes in general anxiety.
- The role of specific rigid and extreme attitudes towards specific threats in specific instances of anxiety.

In order to feel anxious a person needs to think that they are about to face a threat

In order to feel anxious a person needs to think that they are about to face some kind of threat. Without making a threat-related inference, the person won't feel psychologically anxious.

There are two different kinds of threats that a person may experience: threats to ego aspects of their personal domain and threats to non-ego aspects of their personal domain. As Aaron T. Beck (1976) noted in his book *Cognitive Therapy and the Emotional Disorders*,[1] the personal domain includes anything that a person holds dear. So when a person faces an ego threat, they are facing a threat to something that they hold dear, which has an

DOI: 10.4324/9781003203483-2

impact on their self-esteem (e.g. they think that they might fail an examination, and if they did they would consider themself to be a failure). When a person faces a non-ego threat, they are again facing a threat to something that they hold dear, which this time does not have an impact on their self-esteem (e.g. they think that they might feel sick and they contend that they cannot bear experiencing such a feeling).

It is important to note that a threat does not have to be real for a person to feel anxiety. The important point here is that the person themself considers the threat to be real.

A general anxiety-creating philosophy (GAP) underpins general anxiety

While locating a threat is a necessary condition for a person to feel anxious, it is not sufficient for the person to feel anxious. Some people, for example, as we will see, feel concerned rather than anxious about the possibility of facing a threat. In order to experience anxiety about the real and imagined threats in their life, a person needs what I call a 'general anxiety-creating philosophy' (GAP).

There are four ingredients to such a philosophy, which I will review one at a time.

Ingredient 1: A rigid attitude

The first ingredient of a GAP is known as a rigid attitude.

When a person holds a rigid attitude towards threats, they first assert that they prefer that such threats do not exist in the first place nor occur in the second. I call this a 'shared preference' component because this is present in both their rigid attitude and, as we will see in Chapter 2, their flexible attitude. Then, they add an 'asserted demand' component to this preference: 'I would prefer that these threats do not exist or occur and therefore they must not do so.'[2]

For example, Sally is generally anxious about going for a health check and identifies a threat in that category (i.e. discovering that she is ill). Sally's preference is as follows: 'I would much prefer not to be ill', to which she adds her asserted demand: '...and therefore I must not be ill'. By demanding that she must not be ill, Sally experiences the following consequences:

EMOTIONAL CONSEQUENCES

Sally experiences anxiety.

THINKING CONSEQUENCES

Sally's subsequent thinking is skewed and very distorted. She is so preoccupied with the possibility that she is ill that she excludes the possibility that she may be well and all she can think about concerns illness. In other words, Sally has tunnel vision that serves to sustain her anxiety.

BEHAVIOURAL CONSEQUENCES

Sally's behaviour is characterised by avoidance. She avoids going for health checks. This will have the effect of reinforcing her extreme awfulising attitude (to be discussed presently) that it would be absolutely horrible to be ill. If it wasn't horrible, she reasons, she wouldn't avoid going for health checks.

I will discuss the thinking and behavioural consequences of anxiety-related rigid/extreme attitudes more fully later in the chapter.

Rigid attitudes would make sense if they actually removed the possibility of facing a threat. Thus, if by demanding that she must not be ill, Sally removed the possibility of being ill, then making this demand would make sense. However, making demands has no such effect on reality. They don't magically remove the possibility of threats existing.

Ingredient 2: An awfulising attitude

The second ingredient of a GAP is known as an awfulising attitude. When a person holds such an attitude, they first assert that it would be bad for these threats to exist and to occur. I call this a 'shared evaluation of badness' component because this is present in both their awfulising attitude and, as we shall see in Chapter 2, their non-awfulising attitude. Then, they add an 'asserted awfulising' component to this evaluation of badness: 'It is bad for these threats to happen and it would therefore be horrible, awful, terrible or the end of the world for these threats to exist in the first place and for them to occur in the second place.'[3]

Here the person converts their sensible, non-extreme conclusions – e.g. in Sally's case that it would be bad or unfortunate to be ill – into illogical extreme conclusions – therefore it would be absolutely dreadful or the end of the world to be ill.

When Sally holds an awfulising attitude and she thinks of going for health checks, for example, she tells herself that if she was ill, nothing could be worse than this, and if it did happen, absolutely no good could possibly come from such an eventuality.

Ingredient 3: An unbearability attitude

The third ingredient of a GAP is known as an unbearability attitude. When a person holds such an attitude, they first assert that it would be a struggle for them to bear the existence and occurrence of such threats. I call this a 'shared struggle component' because this is present in both their unbearability attitude and, as we shall see in Chapter 2, their bearability attitude. Then they add an 'unbearability' component to this struggle: 'It is a struggle for me to bear the existence and occurrence of these threats and therefore I couldn't bear them.'[4]

Thus, Sally's anxiety is underpinned by her unbearability attitude that it would be unbearable for her to be ill. When she holds this attitude, she pictures herself crumpled up in a heap on being told that she is ill and thinks that she will lose the capacity for happiness if she were ill.

Ingredient 4: A self-devaluation attitude

As mentioned above, there are two basic forms of anxiety: ego anxiety, where a person makes themself anxious about a threat to their self-esteem, and non-ego anxiety, where they make themself anxious about threats to things that do not involve self-esteem. In the latter type of anxiety, non-ego anxiety, a person generally holds a rigid attitude and then either an awfulising attitude or an unbearability attitude is most dominant in their thinking. Putting this diagrammatically we have:

> *Non-ego anxiety = Threat to non-ego aspect of personal domain × rigid attitude + awfulising attitude or unbearability attitude*

In ego anxiety, a person generally holds a rigid attitude and a self-devaluation attitude, as shown below:

Ego anxiety = Threat to ego aspect of personal domain × rigid demand + self-devaluation attitude

When a person holds a self-devaluation attitude, they first evaluate negatively some aspect of themselves or what happened to them. I call this a 'shared negatively evaluated aspect' component because this is present in both their self-devaluation attitude and, as we shall see in Chapter 2, their unconditional self-acceptance attitude. Then they add an 'asserted global negative evaluation of self' component to this 'shared negatively evaluated aspect' component: 'It is bad if these threats exist and occur and if they do this proves that I am a failure, less worthy or unlovable.'[5]

For example, Norman is anxious about receiving disapproval (a general category of events that, if they happened, would result in him lowering his self-esteem). Thus, receiving disapproval is, for Norman, an ego threat. Now if we add Norman's rigid attitude and self-devaluation attitude to this threat, we have: 'I must not be disapproved of and if I am this proves that I am an unlikeable person.'

When a person is anxious in specific situations, they focus on a specific threat and practise a specific version of their general anxiety-creating philosophy

When a person holds a GAP, doing so increases the chances of identifying threats in their environment. This tendency to locate threats to their personal domain is characteristic of a person who experiences general anxiety. If a person only identified such threats when they actually existed, they would still make themself anxious, but wouldn't do so very often. To make themself anxious regularly and frequently, a person tends to be very sensitive to threats to their personal domain. GAPs sensitise a person to the possibility of threat in the absence of objective evidence that such threats actually exist. Let me explain how holding a GAP influences a person's ability to identify threats in their environment.

Norman (whom we met above) holds the following GAP: 'I must be approved by new people that I meet and if I'm not it proves that I am unlikeable.' Since Norman holds this attitude, he will become preoccupied with the possibility that new people will not like him and will think that he is unlikeable, unless he is certain that they will like him. This preoccupation will involve Norman tending to do the following:

8 Anxiety and concern

- He will tend to overestimate the chances that a new group of people won't approve of him and underestimate the chances that they will approve of him (overestimating the *probability* of disapproval).
- He will tend to think that if they do disapprove of him, they will disapprove of him greatly, rather than just mildly or moderately (overestimating the *degree* of disapproval).
- He will tend to think that all or most of those present will disapprove of him rather than the more realistic situation where some might disapprove of him, others might approve of him and yet others might be neutral towards him – assuming that he doesn't have crass social habits that will objectively antagonise all or most people he has just met (overestimating the *extent* of disapproval).

In summary, when a person holds a GAP about approval, for example, they will overestimate the probability, degree and extent of the opposite happening (i.e. being disapproved) in their environment. GAPs lead a person to become oversensitive to threat.

So far I have discussed the role that general anxiety-creating philosophies play in making a person oversensitive to threat in their environment. Once the person has identified a specific threat in a specific environment, they will then hold a specific version of their GAP to make themself anxious in that specific situation. Let's take Norman's example again. He holds a GAP that I discussed above, namely: 'I must be approved by new people that I meet and if I'm not it proves that I am unlikeable.' Now let's further assume that Norman goes to a party where there are people that he doesn't know and his host is about to introduce him to these people. Norman's GAP will immediately lead him to focus on the threat in this situation: 'These specific people will not like me.' This is known as an inference. An inference is a hunch about reality that can be correct or incorrect, but a GAP leads a person to think of it as a fact.

Having focused on this specific threat, Norman needs to hold a specific version of his GAP. In this case, it is: 'These people that I am about to meet must not disapprove of me and if they do it means that I am unlikeable.' Holding this specific attitude and applying it to the threat-related inference will mean that Norman will be anxious in the specific situation under consideration.

Focusing on and going with the behavioural and thinking consequences of rigid/extreme attitudes will serve to maintain anxiety

In summary, holding a general anxiety-creating philosophy will lead a person to seek out threats in their environment and they will make themself anxious about these threats by specific versions of their GAP. Anxiety, then, is the emotional consequence of this threat–rigid/extreme attitude interaction as shown below:

$$\textit{Specific threat} \times \textit{specific rigid/extreme attitude} = \textit{anxiety}$$

However, there are two other consequences of this threat–rigid/extreme attitude interaction that serve to maintain and exacerbate anxiety. These are known as behavioural consequences and thinking consequences.

Behavioural consequences of rigid/extreme attitudes

Let's start with the behavioural consequences of the threat × rigid/extreme attitude interaction. Thus, when Norman thinks that new people he is about to meet will disapprove of him (threat) and he demands that this must not happen and he is unlikeable if it does (rigid/extreme attitude), then he may act or tend to act in a number of ways:

- He may tend to avoid meeting these new people (*avoiding* the threat).
- If Norman has to meet these new people, he may leave at the first opportunity (physically *withdrawing* from the threat).
- If Norman cannot leave the situation, he may remain silent so that he doesn't do anything to provoke disapproval (*passive neutralising* of the threat).
- He may go out of his way to get approval from the people concerned (*active neutralising* of the threat).
- If Norman cannot leave the situation, he may find some way of behaviourally distracting himself from the threat such as picking his hands (*behavioural distraction* from the threat).
- He may try to deal with the threat by overcompensating for it, e.g. by actively provoking disapproval to try to convince himself

that he doesn't care if he is approved or not (*behaviourally over-compensating* for the threat).

If Norman acts in one or more of the above ways, once he is anxious, then he will maintain his anxiety. By acting in such ways, Norman is actually rehearsing and thus strengthening his specific and general rigid/extreme attitudes. Thus, when Norman avoids being introduced to a new group of people, he implicitly thinks something like: 'If I were to meet these people, they might disapprove of me. They must not disapprove of me and if they do it means that I am unlikeable. Thus, I'll avoid meeting them.' And when a person strengthens their rigid/extreme attitudes towards threat, they increase the likelihood that they will make themselves anxious in future.

The following sums up what I have said in this section:

Specific threat × Specific rigid/extreme attitude = Behavioural consequences: Unconstructive
- Avoiding the threat.
- Physically withdrawing from the threat.
- Passive neutralising of the threat.
- Active neutralising of the threat.
- Behavioural distraction from the threat.
- Behaviourally overcompensating for the threat.

Thinking consequences of rigid/extreme attitudes

There are also thinking consequences of the threat–rigid/extreme attitude interaction. These consequences are of two types. The first type I call 'threat-exaggerated thinking'. This involves the person elaborating on the threat. For example, when Norman thinks that new people he is about to meet will disapprove of him (threat) and he demands that this must not happen and he is unlikeable if it does (rigid/extreme attitude), then he will tend to think in a number of ways:

- He will tend to think that the consequences of the disapproval that he predicts that he will receive will be highly negative. Thus, he may think that once the strangers disapprove of him, they will tell others about their negative views of him, that their disapproval of him will last a long time and that it may affect his chances of meeting new friends in the future (*exaggerating the negative consequences* of the predicted threat).

This thinking consequence serves to increase Norman's anxiety because it gives him even more negative threats to think about while holding other specific rigid/extreme attitudes.

The second type of thinking consequences is what I call 'safety-seeking thinking', the purpose of which is designed, in the person's mind, to keep themself safe from the threat. Thus Norman may do the following:

- He may try to distract himself from the threat by attempting to think of something else (*cognitive distraction* from the threat).
- He may attempt to overcompensate for the threat in his thinking either by imagining himself being indifferent to the disapproval or by thinking of himself gaining great approval in another (imaginary) setting (*cognitively overcompensating* for the threat).
- He may try to reassure himself that the people will approve of him.

These two thinking consequences serve to maintain anxiety in ways that are similar to the behavioural consequences I discussed earlier in that they implicitly give the person an opportunity to rehearse and thus strengthen their rigid/extreme attitude. Thus, if Norman tries to distract himself from the possibility that a new group of people will not approve of him, he is largely doing so because he believes implicitly that they must approve of him and he is unlikeable if they don't. If he wasn't holding rigid/extreme attitudes towards this threat, he would be more likely to think about the threat objectively and deal with it constructively if it actually occurred.

To sum up:

Specific threat × *Specific rigid/extreme attitude* = *Thinking consequences: Highly distorted and skewed to the negative*
- Threat-exaggerated thinking.
- Safety-seeking thinking.

The final point I want to make about these two different types of thinking consequences is that a person can alternate between the two. For example, the more a person engages in threat-exaggerated thinking, the more they will tend to seek safety from the threat in their mind. However, because they cannot ultimately convince themselves that they are safe from the threat, the more they will exaggerate it and its consequences.

How a person adds anxious insult to anxious injury

A person may unwittingly increase and deepen their anxiety by holding a specific anxiety-creating attitude towards different aspects of their anxiety. Let me give you an example of what I mean.

Remember that Norman's GAP is: 'I must be approved by new people that I meet and if I'm not it proves that I am unlikeable.' He attends a social gathering where he is likely to be introduced to people that he doesn't know. Under these conditions, his GAP will lead him to identify a specific threat in this situation, namely that strangers at the gathering are likely to disapprove of him. He then brings a specific version of his GAP to this specific threat until he has made himself anxious. Then, and this is the important point, he may focus on some aspect of his anxiety and think about this using another specific anxiety-creating rigid/extreme attitude. Here are some examples of how Norman may unwittingly increase his anxiety in this way:

- *He may focus on his general feelings of anxiety* and tell himself: 'I must not be anxious, I can't stand feeling anxious and I have to get rid of it immediately.' This will increase his feelings of anxiety.
- *He may focus on a symptom of his anxiety* (such as his heart pounding) and tell himself: 'I must stop my heart pounding and it would be terrible if I don't.' This will increase his heart rate further and also make it more likely that he will think he will have a heart attack if his palpitations increase – which they will if he holds such an attitude.
- *He may focus on a behavioural consequence of his anxiety* (e.g. his urge to avoid meeting new people) and tell himself: 'I must not feel like avoiding this situation and because I do I am a weak wimp.'
- *He may focus on a thinking consequence of his anxiety* (e.g. that new people will laugh at me if I say something silly) and tell himself: 'I must not think this and as I am it proves I am stupid.'

As a person keeps increasing their feelings of anxiety, their negative thoughts will become more dire and their urge to act in unconstructive ways will become more pressing. When this happens and they hold a specific rigid/extreme attitude towards each spiral, they will eventually get themself into a state of panic, their thoughts spiralling out of control and becoming ever more chaotic.

Understanding specific forms of anxiety

In this section, I will discuss the following specific forms of anxiety:

- Anxiety about losing self-control.
- Anxiety about uncertainty.
- Health anxiety.
- Social anxiety.
- Panic attacks.

Anxiety about losing self-control

One of the most common themes in people's anxiety concerns losing self-control. This is not surprising since one of the things many of us take pride in is our ability to remain in control of ourselves and in particular of our feelings, our thoughts and our behaviour. When a person makes themself anxious about losing self-control, they hold a rigid attitude towards self-control in the area of their preoccupation. For example:

- 'I must not feel anxious' (loss of self-control over feelings).
- 'I must not think weird thoughts' (loss of self-control over thoughts).
- 'I must not have images that I find hard to dismiss' (loss of self-control over images).
- 'I must not have the urge to act in that way' (loss of self-control over urges to act).
- 'I must behave in a certain way' (loss of self-control over behaviour).

The above tend to be general anxiety-creating rigid attitudes. In a specific situation, a person brings a relevant, specific rigid/extreme attitude to an episode where they have begun to lose a bit of

14 Anxiety and concern

self-control. For example, take the case of Lara, who has started to have an image of throwing herself off a bridge. She tells herself that she must not have such a mental picture and that she must get rid of the image immediately. As a consequence of this rigid attitude, Lara's image becomes more vivid and increases in aversiveness. Then Lara begins to think that unless she gains control of her images right now, she will go mad. She will then tend to avoid situations with which she associates losing control. Thus, she may well avoid going over bridges or even looking at pictures of bridges.

She may also avoid the subject of mental breakdown and pictures of psychiatric hospitals in an attempt to regain emotional control, but as she does so, she unwittingly strengthens her dire need for self-control. After a while, in her mind Lara will quickly jump from the beginning of losing self-control (e.g. beginning to have the image of throwing herself off a bridge) to the end where she has gone crazy. With practice, Lara develops the following rigid attitude with the following thinking consequence: 'I must be in control of my mental processes at all times or I will go mad' (with the unspoken idea that it is terrible to go mad).

In cases of anxiety about losing self-control, people tend to have the idea that their thoughts, feelings and urges to act are a good guide to reality. In Lara's case, if she thinks that she is going to throw herself off a bridge, then she will. Since she thinks that having the image of throwing herself off a bridge means that she is going to do it, in order to make herself safe, she thinks that she mustn't have such an image. Paradoxically, when a person demands that they must not have a thought or an image, then they make it more likely that they will have such a thought or image.

With such a demand, every intensification of the image leads Lara to redouble her demands to get rid of the image and soon all she will be able to think of is throwing herself off a bridge.

Anxiety about uncertainty

Many people make themselves anxious about uncertainty. Let me explain how this works by discussing the case of Cleo.

1   Cleo focuses on something uncertain that constitutes a threat to her (e.g. 'My children are 15 minutes late home and I don't know what has happened to them').

2   Cleo rehearses the attitude that she must be sure that the threat does not exist and that it is awful not to have such certainty (e.g. 'I must know that my children are safe and it is awful not to know this').
3   Cleo practises the idea that uncertainty means that bad things will inevitably occur (e.g. 'Because I don't know that my children are safe and I must know this, not knowing that they are safe means that something bad has happened to them or that they are at risk').
4   Cleo rehearses her awfulising attitude towards this uncertainty (e.g. 'It is awful not knowing that my children are safe').
5   Cleo seeks reassurance from others that the threat really does not exist or she keeps checking to determine that the threat does not exist (e.g. Cleo keeps going to the window to check if she can see her children and she rings round their friends' parents to discover if they know her children's whereabouts).
6   Cleo then casts doubt on such reassurance. (When the parents of Cleo's children's friends try to reassure her that her children are OK, she is immediately reassured, but then she casts doubt on this by saying such things to herself as: 'How do they know?'; 'They are only saying this to reassure me'; 'I'm sure that they would be out of their minds with worry if it was their children who were late').
7   Cleo keeps a mental scrapbook of stories about the bad things that happen to children who are late home and ignores the millions of unreported incidents of children being late home who were safe.

Health anxiety

Health anxiety occurs when a person thinks that they have a serious illness in the absence of convincing evidence to support their contention. In my view, it is a specific form of anxiety about uncertainty. I will use the example of Esther to show health anxiety in action.

1   Esther has the general rigid/extreme attitude that she must know at all times that she does not have a serious disease and that it is terrible if she doesn't have such certainty. This attitude leads Esther to become adept at identifying symptoms that could be signs of serious illness.

2. Esther focuses on a particular symptom that could be evidence of a serious illness (e.g. skin blemishes, lumps and pains). Recently, Esther identified a pain in her chest and brought a specific version of the above-mentioned general rigid/extreme attitude to this specific situation (i.e. 'I must know now that this chest pain is not a sign of a heart attack and I can't bear not knowing this').
3. Esther thought that uncertainty in this context was a sign of serious illness.
4. She sought professional advice and when it was given and she was reassured that there was nothing seriously wrong with her, she cast doubt on this reassurance when her symptom persisted. She could not see that the continuation of her symptom was due to the attention that she gave to it, influenced by her rigid/extreme attitude. Rather, she accepted the view that states that such symptoms are exclusively due to organic, non-psychological symptoms.

People with health anxiety frequently cast doubt on the validity of the medical opinion that they have been given that there is nothing wrong with them. They do so by:

- Doubting the thoroughness of the examination (e.g. 'In retrospect the doctor only gave me a cursory examination and they didn't ask me many questions about my symptoms. I really think that they missed something.').
- Doubting the state of the medical examiner when they conducted the examination (e.g. 'Come to think of it the doctor looked pale and distracted when they were examining me. I really think that they missed something.').
- Doubting the competence of the medical examiner (e.g. 'I've heard a number of people say that the doctor who examined me is incompetent. I really think that they missed something.').

5. Esther consulted other medical examiners and cast doubt on the opinions given each time.
6. Esther asked her family and friends for reassurance, which only had a short-lived effect because she was not reassurable.
7. Esther consulted books on medical symptoms and visited sites on the internet in the hope of finding out that her symptoms were benign. However, she inevitably found something to support the view that she was seriously ill and when she found such information, she accepted it as true, at least in her case.

Understanding anxiety 17

8 Esther kept checking to determine the status of her symptoms, which increased her health anxiety. Checking focused her attention on the symptoms that she was worried about and meant that she became more aware of them. Her increased attention led to an intensification of her symptoms. Then, as she thought her symptoms were getting worse, she brought her awfulising attitude to this situation, which led her to conclude that she must be seriously ill.

There are symptoms such as skin blemishes and lumps that get worse if a person physically checks on them. If the person awfulises about this 'deterioration', they tend to conclude once again that they are seriously ill.

9 Esther acted as though she was seriously ill. Thinking that the chest pains that she had been experiencing meant that she was suffering from a heart condition, she stopped taking exercise and avoided situations that might raise her heart rate.

Social anxiety

Many people are anxious about social situations. Let me explain how this works by discussing the case of Steve.

1 When Steve gets to a relevant social situation, he remembers his ideal social behaviour and focuses on the fact that he will fall far short of such behaviour. Then he demands that he must act in accord with his ideal and that he is a worthless person if he doesn't.

2 He then thinks that others present will judge him negatively, but he doesn't look at them so he can't disconfirm this inference.

3 While thinking that others are judging him negatively, Steve demands that they must not do this and if they do that this proves that he is worthless.

4 If Steve does go to social situations, he tends to keep himself to himself and does not initiate social contact with others. Consequently, he comes across as uninterested in others, who therefore do not attempt to talk to him. Steve focuses on this latter point, does not realise his role in keeping others away and thinks he is worthless because others do not talk to him.

5 If Steve avoids similar social situations in future, he keeps reminding himself that if he did go out socially, he must come across well and he must be liked, otherwise he will be worthless.

6   Largely as a result of his social anxiety, Steve has developed poor social skills. In particular, he does not engage people in appropriate eye contact. He either stares at people for a long period of time or does not engage in eye contact with them at all.

Panic attacks

Panic attacks are a particularly painful form of anxiety. There are three core elements of a panic attack:

- The attitude that a person must not lose control and it is terrible if they do.
- The notion that when the person's symptoms increase, this is evidence that they are facing an imminent internal catastrophe (e.g. a heart attack, a stroke, going mad, fainting, to name but a few).
- The idea that it is terrible to have a panic attack and that the person must avoid doing so at all costs.

Let's take these points one at a time.

The first foundation of a panic attack is an anxiety about anxiety philosophy. Henry is waiting to give a public presentation and notices that he feels somewhat anxious and sweaty. When he tells himself that it is horrific to feel anxious and that he must gain control of it immediately, he then increases his anxiety. If every time Henry's anxiety increases, he awfulises about it, he will begin to feel that he is really losing control. When he gets to this stage, it will be very easy for him to demand that he must gain control immediately and that it will be terrible if he doesn't.

The second foundation of a panic attack involves the inference that an immediate, catastrophic internal event is likely to happen if the person doesn't gain immediate control. Common catastrophic inferences include having a heart attack, having a stroke or going mad in some way. Then the person tends to act in order to avoid such an event happening. For example, when Henry thought that he was going to have a stroke, at the point when he felt as if he was losing control, he sat down to stop himself (i.e. in his mind) from having one. In doing so, Henry calmed down because he thought that his action warded off having a stroke. He did this whenever he felt he was going to have a stroke and, in doing so, Henry never actually tested out the validity of his inference.

The third foundation of a panic attack is for the person to become anxious about having a panic attack. This is likely to happen under the following conditions:

- When the person rehearses the rigid/extreme attitude that they must not experience a panic attack and it would be awful to do so.
- When the person thinks that wherever they go they might have a panic attack and when they practise the above attitude while thinking this.
- When the person avoids going to places where they think that they might have a panic attack.
- When the person takes steps to avoid having a panic attack if they cannot avoid going to such places (e.g. by using medication, drink or drugs).

A view of the world founded on anxiety-creating rigid/extreme attitudes renders a person particularly vulnerable to developing and maintaining anxiety

People develop views of the world as it relates to them that render them vulnerable to particular unhealthy negative emotions. This is certainly the case with anxiety. The world views that render a person vulnerable to anxiety do so primarily because they make it very easy for the person to make anxiety-related inferences. Then the person makes themself anxious about these inferences with the appropriate rigid/extreme attitudes. Here is an illustrative list of world views and the inferences that they spawn.

World view: The world is a dangerous place.
Inference: If a situation can be threatening, then it is threatening.

World view: Uncertainty is dangerous.
Inference: Not knowing that a threat does not exist means that it does.

World view: Not being in control is dangerous.
Inference: If I am not in control, then I will soon lose control completely.

World view: People can't be trusted.
Inference: People are unpredictable and will threaten me without warning.

Having discussed the REBT perspective on anxiety, in the next chapter I will discuss what it has to say about concern, which is the healthy alternative to anxiety.

Notes

1. A.T. Beck (1976) *Cognitive Therapy and the Emotional Disorders.* New York: International Universities Press.
2. In everyday language this is usually expressed as: 'These threats must not exist or occur.'
3. In everyday language this is usually expressed as: 'It would be horrible, awful, terrible or the end of the world for these threats to exist in the first place and for them to occur in the second place.'
4. In everyday language this is usually expressed as: 'I couldn't tolerate the existence and occurrence of these threats.'
5. In everyday language this is usually expressed as: 'I am a failure, less worthy or unlovable if these threats exist or occur.'

Further reading

Academic

Seif, M.N. & Winston, S. (2014). *What every therapist needs to know about anxiety disorders: Key concepts, insights and interventions.* New York: Routledge.

Self-help

Dryden, W. (2011). *Manage your anxiety through CBT.* London: Hodder Education.

Chapter 2

Understanding concern

In this chapter, I will make some general observations about concern before discussing more specific areas of this constructive emotion.

General points about concern

From the perspective taken in REBT, concern is the healthy alternative to anxiety. So, in this section, I will discuss:

- The role of threat in concern.
- The role of a general concern-related philosophy comprising four general flexible and non-extreme attitudes.
- The role of specific flexible and non-extreme attitudes towards specific threats in specific instances of concern.

In order to feel concern a person needs to think that they are about to face a threat

As with anxiety, in order to feel concern a person needs to think that they are about to face some kind of threat. Without making a threat-related inference, the person won't experience concern. As I mentioned in Chapter 1, there are two types of threat: threats to ego aspects of their personal domain and threats to non-ego aspects of their personal domain. A threat does not have to be real for a person to feel concern. The important point here is that the person themself considers the threat to be real.

A general concern-related philosophy (GCP) underpins general concern

While locating a threat is a necessary condition for a person to feel concern, it is not sufficient for the person to feel this emotion. Some people, as we saw in Chapter 1, feel anxious rather than concern about the possibility of facing a threat. In order to experience concern about the real and imagined threats in their life, a person needs what I call a 'general concern-related philosophy' (GCP).

There are four ingredients to such a philosophy, which I will review one at a time.

Ingredient 1: A flexible attitude

The first ingredient of a (GCP is known as a flexible attitude. When a person holds a flexible attitude towards threats, they first assert that they prefer that such threats do not exist in the first place nor occur in the second. As I mentioned in Chapter 1, I call this a 'shared preference' component because this is present in both their rigid attitude and their flexible attitude. Then they add a 'negated demand' component to this preference: 'I would prefer that these threats do not exist or occur, but that does not mean that they must not exist or occur.'

For example, if Sally, whom we met in Chapter 1, was concerned but not anxious about going for a health check, she would still identify a threat in that category (i.e. discovering that she is ill). As we saw in Chapter 1, Sally's preference was as follows: 'I would much prefer not to be ill...', but to be concerned but not anxious she would add her negated demand: 'but that does not mean that I must not be ill'. By preferring not to be ill but not demanding that this must not be the case, Sally experiences the following consequences:

EMOTIONAL CONSEQUENCES

Sally experiences concern.

THINKING CONSEQUENCES

Sally's subsequent thinking is balanced and realistic. She acknowledges that she may be ill, but also entertains the probability that she is well until she has evidence to the contrary.

BEHAVIOURAL CONSEQUENCES

Sally's behaviour is characterised by facing the threat. Thus, she goes for health checks when appropriate, but not for reassurance when this is not objectively needed.

I will discuss the thinking and behavioural consequences of concern-related flexible/non-extreme attitudes more fully later in the chapter.

Flexible attitudes make sense because they make clear a person's preferences without trying to remove the possibility of facing a threat.

Ingredient 2: A non-awfulising attitude

The second ingredient of a GCP is known as a non-awfulising attitude. When a person holds such an attitude, they again first assert that it would be bad for these threats to exist and to occur. As I said in Chapter 1, I call this a 'shared evaluation of badness' component because this is present in both a person's awfulising attitude and their non-awfulising attitude. In concern, the person then adds a 'negated awfulising' component to this evaluation of badness: 'It is bad for these threats to happen, but it would not be horrible, awful, terrible or the end of the world for these threats to exist in the first place and for them to occur in the second place.'

Here the person retains sensible, non-extreme conclusions in their non-awfulising attitude – e.g. in Sally's case, that it would be bad or unfortunate to be ill, but it would not be absolutely dreadful or the end of the world to be ill.

When Sally holds a non-awfulising attitude and she thinks of going for health checks, for example, she tells herself that if she was ill, then she would get treatment and good could possibly come from such an eventuality.

Ingredient 3: A bearability attitude

The third ingredient of a general concern-related philosophy (GCP) is known as a bearability attitude. When a person holds such an attitude, they first assert that it would be a struggle for them to bear the existence and occurrence of such threats. As I mentioned in Chapter 1, I call this a 'shared struggle component' because this is present in both their unbearability attitude and their bearability attitude. Then they add a number of components to this struggle which

I refer to as the 'bearability', 'worth bearing', 'willing to bear' and 'going to bear' components: 'It is a struggle for me to bear the existence and occurrence of these threats, but I can bear them, it is worth it to me to do so, I am willing to bear them and I am going to do so.'

Thus, Sally's concern is underpinned by her bearability attitude that it would be a struggle for her to be ill, but she could bear it, it would be worth it for her to do so and she is both willing to do so and going to do so. When she holds this attitude, she pictures herself struggling on being told that she is ill, but thinks that she still retains the capacity for happiness if she were ill.

Ingredient 4: An unconditional self-acceptance attitude

As mentioned above, there are two basic forms of concern: ego concern, where a person makes themself concerned about a threat to their view of themself, and non-ego anxiety, where they make themself anxious about threats to things that do not involve their self-view. In the latter type of concern, non-ego concern, a person generally holds a flexible attitude and then either a non-awfulising attitude or a bearability attitude is most dominant in their thinking. Putting this diagrammatically we have:

Non-ego concern = Threat to non-ego aspect of personal domain × flexible attitude + non-awfulising attitude or bearability attitude

In ego concern, a person generally holds a flexible attitude and an unconditional self-acceptance attitude as shown below:

Ego concern = Threat to ego aspect of personal domain × flexible attitude + unconditional self-acceptance attitude

When a person holds an unconditional self-acceptance attitude, they first evaluate negatively some aspect of themself or what happened to them. As I explained in Chapter 1, I call this a 'shared negatively evaluated aspect' component because it is present in both the person's self-devaluation attitude and their unconditional self-acceptance attitude. Then they add two components to this 'shared negatively evaluated aspect' component: (a) a 'negated global negative evaluation of self' component and (b) an 'asserted complex fallible component': 'It is bad if these threats exist and occur and if they do this does not prove that I am a failure, less worthy or unlovable. It proves that I am a complex, unrateable human being.'

For example, Norman is concerned about receiving disapproval, which he regards as an ego threat. If we add Norman's flexible attitude and unconditional self-acceptance attitude to this threat, we have: 'I would prefer not to be disapproved of, but it does not follow that I must not be. If I am, this does not prove that I am an unlikeable person. Rather, it proves that I am a complex, fallible person capable of being liked and disliked.'

When a person experiences concern in specific situations, they focus on a specific threat and practise a specific version of their general concern-related philosophy

When a person holds a GCP, doing so means that they only identify threats that clearly exist. They are not, as they are with anxiety, highly sensitive to threats to their personal domain. However, when they do locate a clear threat, then they hold a specific flexible/non-extreme attitude towards it.

Let me explain the effect of holding a GCP on the person with respect to identifying threats in their environment.

Norman (whom we met above) holds the following GCP: 'I want to be approved by new people that I meet, but I don't have to be. If I'm not approved, it does not prove that I am an unlikeable person, it proves that I am a fallible, complex person who is capable of being liked and disliked.' Since Norman holds this, he will become aware of but not preoccupied with the possibility that new people will not like him and will also think that they may like him. He does not need to be certain of being liked to think of both eventualities. This mindset will have the following effect on Norman:

- He will tend to estimate equally the chances that a new group of people won't approve of him and the chances that they will approve of him (estimating the *probability* of disapproval in a balanced way).
- He will tend to think that if they do disapprove of him, they will disapprove of him mildly or moderately rather than greatly (realistically estimating the *degree* of disapproval).
- He will tend to think that some might disapprove of him, others might approve of him and yet others might be neutral towards

him – assuming that he doesn't have crass social habits that will objectively antagonise all or most of the people he has just met (estimating realistically the *extent* of disapproval).

In summary, when a person holds a GCP about approval, for example, they will estimate the probability, degree and extent of the opposite happening (i.e. being disapproved) in their environment in realistic and balanced ways. GCPs lead a person to become realistically aware of threat, but not oversensitive to it.

So far I have discussed the role that general concern-related philosophies play in influencing a person to be realistically aware of but not oversensitive to threat in their environment. Once the person has identified a specific threat in a specific environment, they will then hold a specific version of their GCP to make themself concerned but not anxious in that specific situation. Let's take Norman's example again. He holds a GCP that I discussed above, namely: 'I want to be approved by new people that I meet, but I don't have to be. If I'm not approved, it does not prove that I am an unlikeable person, it proves that I am a fallible, complex person who is capable of being liked and disliked.' Now let's further assume that Norman goes to a party where there are people that he doesn't know and his host is about to introduce him to these people. Norman's GCP will lead him to identify a threat only when it is clear that a person does not like him

If he discovers such a threat, Norman needs to hold a specific version of his GCP. In this case, it is: 'I would prefer this person to like me, but they do not have to do so. If they don't like me, it does not prove I am unlikeable. I am a person whom some people like and others don't. I can accept myself as such.' Holding this specific attitude and applying it to the threat-related inference will mean that Norman will be concerned but not anxious in the specific situation under consideration.

Focusing on and going with the behavioural and thinking consequences of flexible/non-extreme attitudes will serve to maintain concern and to protect the person from anxiety

In summary, holding a general concern-related philosophy will lead a person to identify threats in their environment only when it is clear that they exist, and they will make themself concerned but not anxious about these threats by specific versions of their GCP.

Concern, then, is the emotional consequence of this threat–flexible/non-extreme attitude interaction, as shown below:

Specific threat × *specific flexible/non-extreme attitude* = *concern*

However, there are two other consequences of this threat–flexible/non-extreme attitude interaction that serve to maintain concern. These are the behavioural consequences and thinking consequences that I first discussed for anxiety in Chapter 1.

Behavioural consequences of flexible/non-extreme attitudes

Let's start with the behavioural consequences of the threat × flexible/non-extreme attitude interaction. Thus, when Norman thinks that new people he is about to meet will disapprove of him (threat) and he prefers this not to happen, but does not demand that this must not do so and he does accept himself unconditionally if it does (flexible/non-extreme attitude), then he may act or tend to act in a number of ways:

- He will meet new people (*facing the possibility* of the threat).
- If Norman has to meet these new people, he will stay till the end of the meeting (*physically remaining in the situation* where the threat is present).
- He will speak up at the meeting even if doing so may provoke disapproval (*actively facing* the threat).
- He will not go out of his way to get approval from the people concerned (*refraining from actively neutralising* the threat).
- He will not behaviourally distract himself from the threat (*refraining from behaviourally distracting himself* from the threat).
- He will act normally in the situation (*refraining from behaviourally overcompensating* for the threat).

If Norman acts in one or more of the above ways, once he is concerned but not anxious, then he will maintain his feelings of concern and prevent himself from becoming anxious. By acting in such ways, Norman is actually rehearsing and thus strengthening his specific and general flexible/non-extreme attitudes. Thus, when Norman faces up to being introduced to a new group of people, he implicitly thinks something like: 'If these people disapprove of me, I won't like it, but I don't have to like it. I can accept myself even if they don't like me. However, it is unlikely that they all will disapprove of me. Some might and some won't, so I am not going to avoid meeting them.' And when a person strengthens their flexible/non-extreme attitudes towards threat, they increase the likelihood that they will make themselves concerned but not anxious in future.

The following sums up what I have said in this section:

Specific threat × Specific flexible/non-extreme attitude =
Behavioural consequences: Constructive
- Facing the possibility of encountering the threat.
- Remaining in the situation when the threat occurs.
- Refraining from passively neutralising the threat.
- Refraining from actively neutralising the threat.
- Refraining from engaging in behavioural distraction from the threat.
- Acting normally and refraining from behaviourally overcompensating for the threat.

Thinking consequences of flexible/non-extreme attitudes

There are also thinking consequences of the threat–flexible/non-extreme attitude interaction as expressed below:

Specific threat × Specific flexible/non-extreme attitude =
Thinking consequences: Balanced and realistic

Examples of these balanced and realistic thinking consequences of flexible and non-extreme attitudes are as follows:

- Thinking realistically about the probability of the threat occurring.
- Viewing the threat realistically when it occurs (in images and in words).
- Realistically appraising one's ability to cope with the threat.
- Problem-solving how to deal with the threat if it occurs rather than ruminating about it.
- Engaging in task-relevant thoughts.
- Picturing oneself dealing with the threat in a realistic way.

Understanding specific forms of concern

In this section, I will discuss the following specific forms of concern:

- Concern about losing self-control.
- Concern about uncertainty.
- Health concern.
- Social concern.
- Panic attacks.

Concern about losing self-control: The healthy alternative to anxiety about losing self-control

I mentioned in Chapter 1 that one of the most common themes in people's anxiety concerns losing self-control. When a person experiences concern but is not anxious about losing self-control, they hold a flexible attitude towards self-control in the area of their interest. For example:

- 'I don't want to feel anxious, but that does not mean I must not feel it' (loss of self-control over feelings).
- 'I would rather not think weird thoughts, but I am not immune from doing so and nor do I have to be immune' (loss of self-control over thoughts).
- 'I would prefer not to have images that I find hard to dismiss, but that does not mean that I must not have them' (loss of self-control over images).
- 'I would rather not have the urge to act in that way, but that does not mean that I must not have that urge' (loss of self-control over urges to act).
- 'I would prefer to behave in a certain way, but I don't have to do so' (loss of self-control over behaviour).

The above tend to be general concern-related flexible attitudes. In a specific situation, a person brings a relevant, specific flexible/non-extreme attitude to an episode where they have begun to lose a bit of self-control. For example, take the case of Lara, whom we met in Chapter 1. Remember that she started to have an image of throwing herself off a bridge. If she was concerned but not anxious about this image, she would tell herself that she would prefer not to have such a mental picture, but she doesn't have to get rid of the image immediately. As a consequence of this flexible attitude, Lara's image fades on its own accord over time. Holding this flexible attitude, Lara would not think that it was likely that she would go mad if she had such an image. She would not avoid situations with which she associates having this image and she would not avoid going over bridges or looking at pictures of bridges.

When a person is concerned but not anxious over losing self-control, they do not tend to have the idea that their thoughts, feelings and urges to act are a good guide to reality. In Lara's case, if she thinks that she is going to throw herself off a bridge, then she does not think that she will. She will tend to see it as something that people think from time to time.

Concern about uncertainty: The healthy alternative to anxiety about uncertainty

Most people do not like uncertainty and quite a few make themselves anxious about it, as we saw in Chapter 1. Remember Cleo whom we met in Chapter 1. Cleo was anxious about uncertainty and we considered an example of this with respect to her anxiety about her children being 15 minutes late and her not knowing where they were. Here is how Cleo could have handled this situation if she was concerned but not anxious about it:

1 Once again, Cleo focuses on something uncertain that constitutes a threat to her (e.g. 'My children are 15 minutes late home and I don't know what has happened to them').
2 Cleo rehearses the attitude that she would like to be sure that the threat does not exist, but she does not have to have such immediate assurance and that it is bad but not awful not to have such certainty (e.g. 'I would like to know that my children are safe, but I don't need to know this right now and it is bad but not awful not to know this').
3 Cleo practises the idea that uncertainty means just that, 'uncertainty'. It does not mean that bad things will inevitably occur (e.g. 'Because I don't know that my children are safe and I would like to know this, but don't have to have immediate assurance, not knowing that they are safe certainly does not mean that something bad has happened to them or that they at risk. It might mean this, but it is more likely to mean that they have been delayed').
4 Cleo rehearses her non-awfulising attitude towards uncertainty (e.g. 'It is bad but not awful not knowing that my children are safe').

5   Cleo refrains from seeking reassurance from others that the threat really does not exist, and she refrains from checking to determine that the threat does not exist (e.g. Cleo has an urge to go to the window to check if she can see her children and an urge to ring round their friends' parents to discover if they know her children's whereabouts, but she does not act on either urge).

Health concern: The healthy alternative to health anxiety

As we saw in Chapter 1, health anxiety occurs when a person thinks that they have a serious illness in the absence of convincing evidence to support their contention. In my view, it is a specific form of anxiety about uncertainty. Health concern, by contrast, occurs when the person faces the possibility that they may have a serious illness. In Chapter 1, I used the example of Esther to show health anxiety in action. In this chapter, I will discuss what changes Esther would have to make to experience health concern rather than health anxiety.

1   Esther would have to hold a general flexible/non-extreme attitude that she would like to know at all times that she does not have a serious disease, but she does not need to know this and it is bad but not terrible if she doesn't have such certainty. This attitude would lead Esther to become sensible, but not sensitive, about identifying symptoms that could be signs of serious illness.
2   Esther would not necessarily focus on a particular symptom that could be evidence of a serious illness (e.g. skin blemishes, lumps and pains). If she did, she would bring a specific version of the above-mentioned general flexible/non-extreme attitude to this specific situation. If she had a chest pain, her attitude would be: 'I would like to know now that this chest pain is not a sign of a heart attack, but I don't need to know this. It's a struggle not knowing this, but I can bear doing so and I am going to do so.'
3   Esther thought that uncertainty in this context was a sign of uncertainty and not necessarily a sign of serious illness.
4   She only sought professional advice when it was clear to her and others that she needed to do so and when it was given, she was reassured that there was nothing seriously wrong with her. Because she was reassurable she accepted this professional opinion even when her symptom persisted for a while. She

understood that any continuation of her symptom may be due to the attention that she gave to it. She rejected the view that states that such symptoms are exclusively due to organic, non-psychological symptoms.

People with health concern generally accept the validity of the medical opinion that they have been given that there is nothing wrong with them.

5   As a result, Esther did not consult other medical examiners even when the symptom persisted for a while.
6   Esther did not ask her family and friends for reassurance if the symptom persisted for a while.
7   Esther refrained from consulting books on medical symptoms and from visiting sites on the internet as she knew that it would not be in her healthy best interests to do so.
8   Esther did not keep checking to determine the status of her symptoms.
9   Esther acted as though she was well. Thinking that the chest pains that she had been experiencing did not mean that she was suffering from a heart condition after she was assured that this was not the case, she continued taking exercise and did not avoid situations that might raise her heart rate.

Social concern: The healthy alternative to social anxiety

Many people are concerned but not anxious about social situations. In Chapter 1, I discussed Steve who experienced social anxiety. In this section, I will assume that Steve experienced social concern instead.

1   When Steve gets to a relevant social situation, he remembers his ideal social behaviour and is aware that he may fall far short of such behaviour. He acknowledges that he would like to act in accord with his ideal, but that he does not have to do so. If he doesn't, Steve does not think he is worthless, but unconditionally accepts himself as a fallible person who can sometimes act in an ideal manner, but more frequently does not do so.
2   While he thinks that some people present may judge him negatively, he also thinks that others won't and he looks at people to see what is happening in this regard.
3   When Steve goes to social situations, which he does not avoid, he mixes with others and initiates social contact with others.

Understanding concern 33

Consequently, he comes across as interested in others and is deemed to be approachable.
4   Because he has social concern rather than social anxiety, Steve has developed good social skills. In particular, apart from conversing with others, he engages people in appropriate eye contact.

Concern about the bodily symptoms of anxiety: The healthy alternative to panic attacks

Panic attacks relate to a person's relationship to the bodily symptoms of anxiety. Concern represents a person's healthy relationship with these symptoms. There are three core elements of such concern:

- The attitude that it is preferable for a person not to experience the bodily symptoms of anxiety and the related sense of loss of control, but it does not mean that they must not have these experiences. It is bad if they do, but it is not terrible.
- The notion that when the person's symptoms increase, this is evidence that their anxiety is increasing, rather than that they are facing an imminent internal catastrophe (e.g. a heart attack, a stroke, going mad, fainting, to name but a few).
- The idea that if they did experience a panic attack, it would be painful but bearable, and that the person does not have to avoid doing so at all costs.

Let's take these points one at a time.

The first foundation of a panic attack is an anxiety about anxiety philosophy. The healthy alternative to this is for the person to feel concern about anxiety. We met Henry in Chapter 1 and analysed the factors associated with his panic attacks. In this chapter I will assume that Henry is concerned but not anxious about his anxiety. Henry was waiting to give a public presentation and notices that he feels somewhat anxious and sweaty. He tells himself that it is unfortunate but not horrific to feel anxious and that he does not have to gain control of it immediately. This idea helps him to calm down.

The second foundation of concern about the bodily symptoms of anxiety is that nothing dreadful is likely to happen if the person doesn't gain immediate control. Given this, the person does not act in order to get away from these symptoms. Such symptoms are painful, to be sure, but they are endurable and when the person is concerned

34 Anxiety and concern

but not anxious about them, they are likely to let these feelings be until they go. This is what Henry did.

The third foundation of a panic attack is for the person to become anxious about having a panic attack. The healthy alternative to this is for the person to become concerned but not anxious about this happening under the following conditions. When the person is concerned about this:

- They rehearse the flexible/non-extreme attitude that they would much prefer not to have a panic attack, but that does not mean that they must not experience one, and it would be bad but not awful to do so.
- They are not scared of thinking that they may have a panic attack.
- They do not avoid going to places where they think that they might have a panic attack.
- They do not use medication, drink and drugs to prevent a panic attack.

Paradoxically, when the person does all of the above, they are far less likely to have a panic attack than they would be if they were anxious about having one.

A view of the world founded on concern-related flexible/non-extreme attitudes helps to protect a person against anxiety

People develop views of the world as it relates to them that lead them to experience particular healthy negative emotions. This is certainly the case with concern. The world views that lead a person to feel concern and help protect them against anxiety do so primarily because they lead the person to make threat-related inferences when it is clear that threat exists. Then the person feels concerned about these inferences with the appropriate flexible/non-extreme attitudes. Here is an illustrative list of world views and the inferences that they spawn.

World view: The world can be a dangerous place, but it can also be a safe place.
Inference: If a situation can be threatening, then it may be threatening, but it is not necessarily so.

World view: Uncertainty is uncomfortable, but not inherently dangerous.
Inference: Not knowing that a threat does not exist does not necessarily mean that it does.

World view: Not being in control is uncomfortable, but not inherently dangerous.
Inference: If I am not in control, then if I adopt a flexible/non-extreme attitude towards this, I will soon regain control.

World view: Some people can't be trusted, but others can.
Inference: Some people are unpredictable and some of these may threaten me without warning. However, being unpredictable does not mean that such people will threaten me, and most others, particularly those who are predictable, pose no or little threat to me.

In the next part of the book, I will discuss depression and its healthy alternative, sadness.

Part 2

Depression and sadness

Chapter 3

Understanding depression[1]

It is useful to distinguish between two types of depression: sociotropic depression and autonomous depression. In sociotropic depression a person is depressed about issues such as loss of affiliation, loss of love, loss of being connected to people and loss of relationships, whereas in autonomous depression a person is depressed about losses of freedom, autonomy, competence and status. Please note from this that loss is a major inference theme in depression, but this is also the case with the healthy alternative to depression, which is sadness. The REBT position is, as we have seen, that depression stems from rigid/extreme attitudes towards loss, while sadness stems from flexible/non-extreme attitudes towards loss. I will first discuss sociotropic depression, before turning my attention to autonomous depression.

Sociotropic depression

In discussing sociotropic depression, I will consider:

- The role of general rigid/extreme attitudes.
- The impact of these attitudes on thinking about loss.
- Specific loss and specific rigid/extreme attitudes.
- The effect of rigid/extreme attitudes on behaviour and subsequent thinking.
- Metaphors and images in sociotropic depression.

The role of general rigid/extreme attitudes in sociotropic depression

When a person makes themselves sociotropically depressed, they tend to hold a number of general rigid/extreme attitudes.

DOI: 10.4324/9781003203483-5

First, they tend to hold *a rigid attitude* towards being liked, loved, connected to people in their life and the role that relationships play for them. In the following list, I will provide both the preference component and the asserted demand component of a rigid attitude. The attitudes in round brackets show how each attitude is commonly expressed in everyday life.

- 'I want to be liked and therefore I have to be liked.' ('I must be liked.')
- 'I want to be loved and therefore I have to be loved.' ('I must be loved.')
- 'I want to be connected to people I care for and therefore I have to be connected to them.' ('I must be connected to people that I care for.')
- 'I want to have a special relationship in my life and therefore I have to have one.' ('I must have a special relationship in my life.')

Second, in some forms of sociotropic depression, a person tends to hold an extreme *self-devaluation attitude* towards these issues. I call this type of depression 'self-worth sociotropic depression' because in effect the person is basing their self-esteem on the presence of being liked, loved, etc. In the following examples, I show the rigid attitudes in square brackets and then list the self-devaluation attitudes that stem from these fixed ideas:

- '[I must be liked]...and if I'm not, then I'm unlikeable.'
- '[I must be loved]...and if I'm not, then I'm unlovable.'
- '[I must be connected to people that I care about]...and if I'm not, then I am not worth caring about.'
- '[I must have a special relationship in my life]...and if I don't, then I'm a nobody.'

Third, in other forms of sociotropic depression (which I call 'discomfort-related sociotropic depression'), the person is not devaluing themselves. Rather, they are disturbing themselves about the resultant conditions that exist following their loss. For example:

- '[I must be liked]...and if I'm not, I couldn't bear it.'
- '[I must be loved]...and if I'm not, it's awful.'

- '[I must be connected to people that I care about]...and if I'm not, then I would disintegrate since I am too weak to look after myself.'
- '[I must have a special relationship in my life]...and if I don't, my life is nothing.'

As can be seen, some of these attitudes are dependency-related attitudes, which are a major feature of sociotropic depression that does not relate to self-worth.

Focusing on sociotropic loss

If a person holds general rigid/extreme attitudes towards loss with respect to being liked, loved, etc. and these are triggered in some way, they will tend to lead the person to focus on such loss in their mind. Such a loss can be a past loss where the person recalls from memory a specific time when they thought they were rejected, disliked or disconnected. Or alternatively, the person can review their present relationships and focus on one which isn't going too well, and then bring a relevant rigid/extreme attitude to this relationship until they conclude that the other person doesn't like them, doesn't love them or wants to reject them.

Bringing a specific rigid/extreme attitude to a specific sociotropic loss

Once a person has focused on a loss and made themself depressed about it, the person has brought a specific version of their general rigid/extreme attitude to this loss. For example, Beryl identified a recent situation where she thought Rosemary, a friend, acted coolly towards her. Using her general rigid/extreme attitude – 'My friends must always show interest in me and if they don't, it proves that I am an unlikeable person' – she translated this 'cool action' into the inference that Rosemary rejected her. Focusing on this specific loss, Beryl brought to it a specific version of her general attitude, namely: 'Rosemary must not reject me and because she did, I am an unlikeable person.'

The same process occurs when a person experiences an actual sociotropic loss. They focus on this loss while holding a specific rigid/extreme attitude and in this way make themself sociotropically depressed.

The effects of rigid/extreme attitudes towards sociotropic loss on behaviour

When a person feels sociotropically depressed, the rigid/extreme attitudes that underpin their depression impact on their behaviour. In other words, a person will tend to act in ways that are consistent with these attitudes and depressed mood. In Beryl's example:

- She avoided Rosemary and other friends.
- She stayed away from enjoyable activities.
- She played depressing music, read depressing novels or poetry (particularly those that deal with rejection).
- She talked to people who were also depressed.

In short, such behaviour is unconstructive.

The effects of rigid/extreme attitudes towards sociotropic loss on subsequent thinking

Depression-related rigid/extreme attitudes have a decided negative effect on a person's subsequent thinking. This thinking becomes highly distorted in negative ways and ruminative. Let me outline and exemplify some of the thinking errors that *stem from* or *follow from* Beryl's specific rigid/extreme attitude: 'Rosemary must not reject me and because she did, I am an unlikeable person.' These thinking errors had a deepening effect on Beryl's depression. In outlining these thinking errors, I will show how they stem from the rigid/extreme attitudes in the underlined text.

- *Black and white thinking* (taking an event and putting it into one of two black and white categories): 'You either like me or you dislike me. There is no other way of looking at it. Since Rosemary has rejected me on this occasion, as she absolutely should not have done, this means that she doesn't like me.'
- *Overgeneralisation* (taking an event and generalising it to all other similar situations and relevant categories): 'Since Rosemary rejected me, as she absolutely should not have done, all my friends will reject me.'
- *Always–never thinking* (taking an event and thinking that it will be like this forever or it will never change): 'Since Rosemary rejected me, as she absolutely should not have done, I'll never

Understanding depression   43

be friends with Rosemary again. I'll always be rejected by my friends.'
- *Exaggeration* (using an event as a springboard to make extreme and exaggerated statements about it and matters relating to it): 'Since Rosemary rejected me, <u>as she absolutely should not have done</u>, nobody truly likes me.'
- *Negative prediction* (taking an event and making negative predictions about it and matters relating to it): 'Since Rosemary rejected me, <u>as she absolutely should not have done</u>, whoever I make friends with in the future will reject me.'
- *Ignoring the positive* (taking an event and making that event colour everything in one's life so that the positive is ignored): 'The fact that I got a good review at work doesn't matter. The only thing that matters is that Rosemary has rejected me, as <u>she absolutely should not have done</u>.'
- *Helplessness* (editing out one's personal resourcefulness to change matters on a broad scale): 'Since Rosemary rejected me, <u>as she absolutely should not have done</u>, I can't do anything to get people to like me. They are capable of liking me, but I don't have the resources to get them to like me.'
- *Hopelessness* (seeing no hope for the future): 'Since Rosemary rejected me, <u>as she absolutely should not have done</u>, I'll be emotionally alone in the future. I have the resources to change matters, but they just can't be changed.'

A particularly potent combination of thinking errors in the deepening of depression is helplessness and hopelessness. In this context, a person shows themself that they do not have the resources to get people to like them (helplessness) and even if they did, it wouldn't change anything (hopelessness).

Bringing rigid/extreme attitudes to subsequent thinking

Once a person has created a particular thinking error by holding a specific rigid/extreme depression-related attitude towards a loss, they may then deepen their depression by focusing on the content of their thinking error from the perspective of another specific rigid/extreme attitude. For example, Beryl created the following thinking error and is now focusing on it: 'Whoever I make friends with in the future will reject me.' She brings the following rigid/extreme attitude to this error, thus: 'People must not keep rejecting me and if they do, it proves that I am completely worthless.'

What will, in all probability, happen is that the person's subsequent thinking will be even more negative and distorted, e.g. 'I will always be alone. I will never be connected to another human being again. Life will always be bleak and hopeless.' This will lead to increased hopelessness about the future.

Metaphors and images in sociotropic depression

When a person is in a sociotropic depression, they will tend to create and dwell on images or metaphors that illustrate how they feel. Here are some examples of such images and metaphors that depict the hopelessness of sociotropic depression:

- 'I am in solitary isolation with no way out.'
- 'I see others enjoying themselves and I have no way of reaching them.'
- 'I am trapped in a loveless existence.'

If the person rehearses such metaphors and images, they will maintain and even deepen their sense of hopelessness.

Autonomous depression

As I pointed out earlier in this chapter, there are two types of depression: sociotropic depression and autonomous depression. If you recall, in sociotropic depression the person is depressed about issues such as loss of affiliation, loss of love, loss of being connected to people and loss of relationships, whereas in autonomous depression the person is depressed about losses of freedom, autonomy, competence and status. In this section, I will discuss autonomous depression.

The role of general rigid/extreme attitudes in autonomous depression

When a person makes themselves autonomously depressed, they tend to hold a number of general rigid/extreme attitudes.

First, they tend to hold a *rigid attitude* towards the place of achieving key goals and standards in their life such as achievement, being competent, self-reliant, autonomous and having high status. In the following list, I will once again provide both the preference component and the asserted demand component of a rigid attitude. The attitudes in round brackets show how each attitude is commonly expressed in everyday life.

- 'I want to achieve important goals in life and therefore I must achieve them.' ('I must achieve important life goals.')
- 'I want to be competent and therefore I must be so.' ('I must be competent.')
- 'I want to be able to determine my life path free from external restrictions and therefore I must do so.' ('I must be able to determine my life path free from external restrictions.')
- 'I want to be self-reliant and therefore I must be so.' ('I must be self-reliant.')
- 'I want to achieve a set status in life and therefore I have to do so.' ('I must achieve a set status in life.')

Second, in some forms of autonomous depression, the person tends to hold a *self-devaluation attitude* towards these issues. I call this type of depression 'self-worth autonomous depression' because in effect the person is basing their self-esteem on the presence of conditions such as achievement, competence, self-reliance, autonomy and status. In the following examples, I show the rigid attitudes in square brackets and then list the self-devaluation attitudes that stem from these fixed ideas:

- '[I must achieve what I want in life]...and if I don't, then I am a failure.'
- '[I must be competent]...and if I'm not, then I am an idiot.'
- '[I must be able to determine my life path free from external restrictions]...and if I can't, then I am a useless person.'
- '[I must be self-reliant]...and if I'm not, then I am a weak person.'
- '[I must achieve the status in life that I set for myself]...and if I don't, then I am worthless.'

Third, in other forms of autonomous depression (which I call 'non-self-worth autonomous depression'), the person is not devaluing themself. Rather, they are disturbing themself about the resultant conditions that exist following their loss.

46 Depression and sadness

- '[I must achieve what I want in life]...and if I don't, I couldn't bear it.'
- '[I must be competent]...and if I'm not, it's awful.'
- '[I must be able to determine my life path free from external restrictions]...and if I am not able to, it's unbearable.'
- '[I must be self-reliant]...and it's the end of the world if I'm not.'
- '[I must achieve the status in life that I have set for myself]...and if I don't, I couldn't stand it.'

Focusing on autonomous loss

If a person holds general rigid/extreme attitudes towards loss with respect to failing, being constrained, losing status, etc. and these are triggered in some way, they will tend to lead the person to focus on such loss in their mind. Thus, as in sociotropic depression, the person's specific autonomous loss can be a past loss where they recall from memory a specific time when they were or thought they were incompetent or controlled by others. Or alternatively they can review their present life and focus on an autonomous area which isn't going too well, and then evaluate this situation with a relevant rigid/extreme attitude as detailed above until they conclude that they have experienced a significant loss.

Bringing a specific rigid/extreme attitude to a specific autonomous loss

Once a person has focused on an autonomous loss and has made themself depressed about it, the person has brought a specific version of their general rigid/extreme attitude to this loss. Thus, Edwina identified a recent situation where she had been taken off a project at work by her boss. Using her general rigid/extreme attitude – 'I must be able to determine my fate and it's terrible if I can't' – she translated being taken off the project into the inference that her fate was being determined by her boss. Focusing on this specific loss, Edwina brought to it a specific version of her general attitude, namely: 'My boss must not determine my fate and it's terrible if he does.'

The effects of rigid/extreme attitudes towards autonomous loss on behaviour

When a person feels autonomously depressed, the rigid/extreme attitudes that underpin this depression impact on their behaviour.

In other words, a person will tend to act in unconstructive ways that are consistent with these attitudes and their depressed mood. In Edwina's example:

- She avoided seeing her boss in order to present a case for remaining on the project.
- She gave up working on other projects to which she had been assigned.
- She played depressing music, read depressing novels or poetry (especially those where the protagonists are constrained).
- She talked to people who were also depressed about how their bosses determine what they do at work.

The effects of rigid/extreme attitudes towards autonomous loss on subsequent thinking

As I said earlier, depression-related rigid/extreme attitudes influence a person's subsequent thinking in that it becomes highly distorted in negative ways and ruminative in nature. These thinking errors will serve to deepen depression. Let me show the types of thinking that *stem from* Edwina's specific autonomous depression-related rigid/extreme attitude: 'My boss must not determine my fate and it's terrible if he does.' These thinking errors had a deepening effect on Edwina's depression. In outlining these thinking errors, I will show how they stem from the rigid/extreme attitudes in underlined text.

- *Black and white thinking* (taking an event and putting it into one of two black and white categories): 'Since my boss has taken me off the project, which he absolutely should not have done, he is completely in control of my destiny since I am either in control of my fate or I am controlled by another person.'
- *Overgeneralisation* (taking an event and generalising it to all other similar situations and relevant categories): 'Since my boss is in control of my destiny in this situation, which he absolutely should not be, he is in control of my destiny in all work-related situations.'
- *Always–never thinking* (taking an event and thinking that it will be like this forever or it will never change): 'Since my boss has taken me off the project, which he absolutely should not have done, I'll never be in charge of my fate again. I'll always be under the control of this boss and other bosses.'

48 Depression and sadness

- *Exaggeration* (using an event as a springboard to make extreme and exaggerated statements about it and matters relating to it): 'Since my boss has taken me off the project, which he absolutely should not have done, my life is ruined if I don't have complete control of my fate, which I must have.'
- *Negative prediction* (taking an event and making negative predictions about it and matters relating to it): 'Since my boss has taken me off the project, which he absolutely should not have done, wherever I work, my destiny will not be my own.'
- *Ignoring the positive* (taking an event and making that event colour everything in one's life so that one ignores the positive): 'The fact that there are other areas of work where I do have control does not matter. The only thing that matters is that my boss has taken me off the project, which he absolutely should not have done.'
- *Helplessness* (editing out one's personal resourcefulness to change matters on a broad scale): 'Since my boss has taken me off the project, which he absolutely should not have done, I can't do anything to change this. Something could be done about it, but I don't have the resources to do it.'
- *Hopelessness* (seeing no hope for the future): 'Since my boss has taken me off the project, which he absolutely should not have done, no matter what happens, others will be in charge of my fate. I have the resources to change matters, but they can't be changed.'

As before, the last two thinking errors represent a particularly potent combination in the deepening of depression.

Bringing rigid/extreme attitudes to subsequent thinking

Once a person has created a particular thinking error by holding a specific rigid/extreme depression-related attitude towards an autonomous loss, they may then deepen their depression by focusing on the content of their thinking error from the perspective of another specific rigid/extreme attitude. For example, Edwina created the following thinking error and is now focusing on it: 'Wherever I work, my destiny will not be my own.' She brings the following rigid/extreme attitude to this error: 'Wherever I work, my destiny must be my own and if it's not, it is completely unbearable.'

What will in all probability happen is that the person's subsequent thinking will be even more negative and distorted, e.g. 'I won't be able to control my destiny in life. Life will always be bleak and hopeless.' This will lead to increased hopelessness about the future.

Metaphors and images in autonomous depression

When a person is in an autonomously depressed frame of mind, they will tend to create and dwell on images or metaphors that illustrate how they feel. Here are some examples of such images and metaphors that depict the hopelessness of autonomous depression:

- 'My life is full of failure and defeat.'
- 'I see others succeeding and reaching their goals, but I have no chance of doing likewise.'
- 'I am a puppet and other people are pulling my strings.'
- 'I see myself in a nightmare where I can't look after myself, so others have to look after me.'

If the person rehearses such metaphors and images, then they will maintain and even deepen their sense of hopelessness.

How depression deepens: The interaction of sociotropic and autonomous depression

I have now explained sociotropic and autonomous depression from an REBT perspective. This knowledge can be used to understand the deepening of depression when these two different types interact.

How a person can make themselves autonomously depressed after they have made themselves sociotropically depressed

Starting with sociotropic depression, let me show how a person can use this type of depression to make themself autonomously depressed as well. Let's take the case of Ralph. He thought that his boss was annoyed with him and he made himself sociotropically depressed about this because he brought the following specific rigid/extreme attitude to this presumed annoyance: 'My boss must not be annoyed with me and if she is, then this proves that I am unlikeable.' As I showed earlier in this chapter, holding a sociotropic depression-related rigid/extreme attitude leads a person to think in ways that are negative and distorted in nature. The *content* of the thinking errors listed in that section that stem from sociotropic depression-related rigid/extreme attitudes is sociotropic in nature. Thus, in the example that I am using here, when Ralph's boss, in his mind, demonstrated annoyance at him and he believed that she must not be annoyed at him and he is unlikeable if she is, he is likely to have such thoughts as: 'If my boss is annoyed at me, others will be too', which are sociotropic in content.

For a person to make themself depressed autonomously after they have made themself depressed sociotropically, they first need to make the thinking that stems from their sociotropic depression-related rigid/extreme attitude autonomous in nature. Thus, if Ralph holds that his boss must not be annoyed with him and he is unlikeable if they are, then when he focuses on his boss being annoyed at him, an example of an autonomous-related thinking consequence of this attitude is: 'I will not advance in my career if my boss is annoyed with me.'

If Ralph then focuses on this distorted autonomous thought, treats it as if it were true and brings an autonomously related rigid/ extreme attitude to it, such as 'I must advance in my career and it's terrible if I don't', doing so will have the following effects:

- Ralph will feel autonomously depressed (don't forget that he already feels sociotropically depressed).
- Subsequently, he will tend to think such distorted autonomous-related thoughts as: 'There's no point in me working hard since I will never advance in my career.'
- He will tend to give up working hard at work, thereby increasing the chances of not getting promoted.

How a person can make themself sociotropically depressed after they have made themself autonomously depressed

Now let me show how a person can make themself sociotropically depressed after they have made themself autonomously depressed. Let's take the case of Derek, who thinks he is struggling at work. He makes himself autonomously depressed about this because he brings the following attitude to this 'struggle': 'I must always do well at work and if I don't, then I am a failure.' Again, holding an autonomous depression-related rigid/extreme attitude will lead a person

Understanding depression 51

to think subsequently in ways that are negative and distorted in nature, and the content of such thinking will be largely autonomous. Derek's subsequent autonomous-based thinking was: 'Because I am struggling at work, I'll lose my job.'

For a person to make themself depressed sociotropically after they have made themself depressed autonomously, they first need to make the thinking that stems from their autonomous depression-related rigid/extreme attitude sociotropic in nature. Thus, if Derek holds that he must always do well at work and he is a failure if he doesn't, then when he focuses on struggling at work, an example of a sociotropic-related thinking consequence of this attitude is: 'My work colleagues will shun me once they see that I am struggling.'

If Derek then focuses on this distorted sociotropic thought, treats it as if it were true and brings a sociotropically related rigid/extreme attitude to it, such as: 'I must have good relations with my work colleagues and if I don't, then I am unlikeable', doing so will have the following effects:

- Derek will feel sociotropically depressed (don't forget that he already feels autonomously depressed).
- Subsequently, he will tend to think such distorted sociotropic-related thoughts as: 'If my work colleagues don't want to know me, nobody will want to know me.'
- He will tend to withdraw socially, thereby increasing the chances of losing contact with people and of thinking that nobody wants to know him.

Self- and other-pity

Self- and other-pity are key components in some forms of depression. Let me consider these one at a time.

Self-pity

When a person feels sorry for themself (rather than for the bad position that they are in), the following tends to happen:

1   The person tends to focus on an aspect of their life where they consider that they have been treated badly or where they have failed to achieve something that they have worked very hard for. In particular, this aspect tends to be one where the person

clearly thinks that (a) they did not deserve the bad treatment and (b) they deserved to achieve what they were striving for. In addition, the person is more likely to experience self-pity in these selected aspects where, in the first case, others who in their view deserved bad treatment actually received good treatment and where, in the second case, others who in their view had not worked as hard as them achieved what they wanted to achieve.

2   The person tends to bring the following rigid/extreme attitude to these inferences at A (which may or may not be accurate):
  - 'I must not be treated badly when I don't deserve to be (and when others who do deserve to be treated badly aren't) and when this occurs (a) it's terrible and (b) the world is a rotten place for allowing this to happen to a poor undeserving person like me.'
  - 'When I work hard for something, I must get what I think I deserve (particularly when others, who don't deserve to, get what I should have got) and when I don't (a) it's terrible and (b) the world is a rotten place for allowing this to happen to a poor undeserving person like me.'

3   These rigid/extreme attitudes tend to influence the person's subsequent thinking. As I have already shown in this book, once a person brings a rigid/extreme attitude to a threat to or a loss from their personal domain, this attitude influences their subsequent thinking in highly distorted negative ways.

Thus, when a person thinks that they have undeservedly been treated badly and they hold a rigid/extreme attitude towards this as shown in (a) above, then they will tend to:
  - Think about all the other occasions where they have been treated badly when they have not merited such treatment.
  - Focus on all the unfairnesses that they have suffered and edit out all the unfairnesses that have been in their favour (which they probably think of as fairnesses).

When the person has worked hard for something and hasn't been awarded it and others less deserving of the award have received it, and they hold a rigid/extreme attitude towards this as detailed in (b) above, then they will tend to:
  - Think about all the other occasions when all their hard work failed to be rewarded and edit out all the occasions when they have been rewarded for working hard as well as occasions when they were rewarded for not working particularly hard.

- Think about all the occasions when others have been rewarded for not working particularly hard and edit out occasions when their hard labours or efforts have also not been rewarded.

  The person can then bring further rigid/extreme attitudes to these distorted thoughts to deepen their 'poor me' depression even further.
4 The person tends to seek out people who are likely to share their 'unhealthy' views about unfairness and tells them about their hard luck story. In all probability, these other people will respond with statements containing or implying rigid/extreme attitudes (e.g. 'Oh my God, poor you; how terrible for you'). Then, the person will probably react to such statements positively because they validate their own way of looking at things and will tend to use such 'other-pity' statements to strengthen their conviction in their self-pity related rigid/extreme attitudes.

Other-pity

When a person feels sorry for others (rather than for their plight), the following tends to happen:

1 The person focuses on an aspect of life where they consider that other people are being treated very badly through no fault of their own. Other-pity is particularly experienced where these other people are clearly helpless victims (e.g. cruelty or abusive behaviour towards a child).
2 The person tends to bring the following rigid/extreme attitude to these inferences at *A* (which may or may not be accurate):
   - 'The world must not allow such bad treatment to happen and because it does, the world is a rotten place. It is the end of the world for such treatment to be meted out to the poor person (or people)'.
3 These rigid/extreme attitudes tend to influence the person's subsequent thinking. Thus, when they think that others have been treated badly through no fault of their own and the person holds a rigid/extreme attitude towards this (as shown above), then they will tend to:
   - Focus on all the unfairnesses and bad treatment that innocent 'victims' have had to endure and edit out all the fairnesses that others have benefited from. In short, the person focuses

on man's inhumanity to man and edits out man's humanity to man. If the person keeps a scrapbook of such inhumane treatment and records news stories and documentaries of this ilk, they will reinforce this biased view of the world.
- Think that the world is getting worse in this respect and that there is no hope for humankind.

The person will then tend to bring further rigid/extreme attitudes to these distorted thoughts to deepen their 'other-pity' depression even further.

4   They will tend, once again, to seek out people who are likely to share their 'unhealthy' views about the 'absolute horror' and 'unbearability' of man's inhumanity to man or swap 'horror' stories with them. These others' unhealthy responses will tend to confirm the person's attitude that the world is a horrible place and reinforce their biased view of the world.
5   The person will tend to be passive and complain externally and internally about how horrible the world is, rather than doing anything practical that might help these innocent 'victims'.

Depression about depression

As humans, we have the ability not only to disturb ourselves, but to disturb ourselves about our disturbances. There are many ways that a person can depress themself about their depression and in this part of the chapter I will cover two main ways.

How a person can depress themself about the physical aspects of depression

Depression can be physically painful. A person may, for example, have difficulty sleeping, may lose their appetite and may have physical aches and pains.

When a person further depresses themself about the physical aspects of their depression, they tend to:

- Focus on the physical aspects of their depression.
- Bring the following rigid/extreme attitude to these aspects: 'I must not feel so bad and I can't bear doing so'.
- Engage in the behavioural and thinking consequences of this attitude:

Behavioural consequence: Remain inert and don't do anything enjoyable. This will have the effect of having the person focus even more on the increased physical pain of their deepening depression.
Thinking consequence: 'I'll never get over this pain. It is just unremitting.'

Self-devaluation about depression

A person can devalue themself about depressing themself in the first place in a number of ways. I will group these ways together.

- The person focuses on what being depressed means for them, e.g. a weakness, a failing, evidence of having an unlovable trait.
- They then bring to this inference one of the following rigid/ extreme attitudes and engage in the illustrative behavioural and thinking consequences of this attitude.

'I must not be weak (by being depressed) and the fact that I have such a weakness means that I am a weak person.'
Behavioural consequence: Hides away from people.
Thinking consequence: Thinks of past instances when they have been weak. Thinks that they will always be weak.

'Being depressed means that I am failing and I must not fail in this respect, and the fact that I have failed proves that I am a failure.'
Behavioural consequence: Doesn't try anything in case they fail.
Thinking consequence: Focuses on past failures. Thinks that they will always fail.

'Being depressed demonstrates that I have an unlovable trait that I must not have. Because I have, it proves that I am an unlovable person'
Behavioural consequence: Stays away from loved ones when depressed; tries to put on a brave face when with loved ones.
Thinking consequence: Thinks that they are bound to be rejected by anyone that they care for if that person sees that they are depressed.

People develop and rehearse a view of the world founded on depression-based rigid/extreme attitudes

I mentioned in the previous chapter that people develop world views that render them vulnerable to particular unhealthy negative emotions. This is certainly the case with depression. The world views that render a person vulnerable to depression do so primarily because they make it very easy for them to make unhealthy depression-related inferences. Then, as I have shown earlier in the chapter, the person makes themself depressed about these inferences with the relevant rigid/extreme attitudes. Here is an illustrative list of world views that a person may develop and rehearse and the inferences that they spawn.

World view: Life is meaningless.
Inference: No matter what I do, ultimately it is meaningless.

World view: People will ultimately reject me.
Inference: If people get to know the real me, they will reject me.

World view: The world is made up of strong and weak people.
Inference: If I am not strong and independent, I am weak and dependent.

Preparing the ground for depression

Depression is very much experienced physically and therefore, in order for a person to feel depressed, they will unwittingly tend to prepare the ground so that their depressed feelings take root. If a person does the following, they will make themself particularly vulnerable to depression:

- They do not wash and walk around all day wearing only their pyjamas/nightgown.
- They read only the bad news in daily newspapers.
- They play as many songs written by Leonard Cohen, or by others specialising in what I call the 'music of misery', as they can find.
- They withdraw from any events that they are likely to enjoy. They only attend events where there is a very good chance of feeling

depressed, either during the event or after it is finished. Even if the person does enjoy the event, they point out to themself that they used to enjoy such events a lot more.
- They do things that they are likely to fail at and avoid doing things that they are likely to be successful at. If they do succeed at anything, they point out to themself that either (a) they used to do such things much better than they do now and/or (b) if they can do it, then anybody can do it.

Having discussed the REBT perspective on depression, in the next chapter I will discuss what it has to say about sadness, which is the healthy alternative to depression.

Note

1 In this book, I am only dealing with non-biological depression that results from psychological factors and does not require the use of medication.

Further reading

Academic

Gotlib, I.H. & Hammen, C. (Eds.) (2017). *Handbook of depression.* 3rd edition. New York: Guilford.

Self-help

Dryden, W. & Opie, S. (2003). *Overcoming depression.* London: Sheldon.

Chapter 4

Understanding sadness

Sadness is the healthy alternative to depression when the person is facing loss, failure or undeserved plight experienced by self or others. It is useful to distinguish between two types of sadness: sociotropic sadness and autonomous sadness. In sociotropic sadness a person experiences sadness about issues such as loss of affiliation, loss of love, loss of being connected to people and loss of relationships, whereas in autonomous sadness a person is sad about losses of freedom, autonomy, competence and status. As we saw in Chapter 3, loss is a major inference theme in both sadness and depression. The REBT position is, as we have seen, that sadness stems from flexible/non-extreme attitudes towards loss. I will first discuss sociotropic sadness, before turning my attention to autonomous sadness.

Sociotropic sadness

In discussing sociotropic sadness, I will consider:

- The role of general flexible/non-extreme attitudes.
- The impact of these attitudes on thinking about loss.
- Specific loss and specific flexible/non-extreme attitudes.
- The effect of flexible/non-extreme attitudes on behaviour and subsequent thinking.
- Metaphors and images in sociotropic sadness.

The role of general flexible/non-extreme attitudes in sociotropic sadness

When a person is sociotropically sad, they tend to hold a number of general flexible/non-extreme attitudes.

DOI: 10.4324/9781003203483-6

First, they tend to hold *a flexible attitude* towards being liked, loved, connected to people in their life and the role that relationships play for them. In the following list, I will provide both the preference component and the negated demand component of a flexible attitude. The attitudes in round brackets show how each attitude is commonly expressed in everyday life.

- 'I want to be liked, but I don't have to be liked.' ('I don't have to be liked.')
- 'I want to be loved, I don't have to be loved.' ('I don't have to loved.')
- 'I want to be connected to people I care for, but I don't have to be so connected.' ('I don't have to be connected to people that I care for.')
- 'I want to have a special relationship in my life, but I don't have to have one.' ('I don't have to have a special relationship in my life.')

Second, in some forms of sociotropic sadness, a person tends to hold a non-extreme *unconditional self-acceptance attitude* towards these issues. I call this type of sadness 'self-acceptance sociotropic sadness' because the person does not base their self-esteem on the presence of being liked, loved, etc. In the following examples, I show the flexible attitudes in square brackets and then list the unconditional self-acceptance attitudes that stem from these fluid ideas:

- '[I want to be liked, but I don't have to be liked]…and if I'm not, then it's not good, but I can accept myself.'
- '[I want to loved, but I don't have to be]…and if I'm not, then I can accept myself as someone who can be loved and not loved.'
- '[I want to be connected to people that I care about, but I don't have to be]…and if I'm not, then I am still worth caring about.'
- '[I want to have a special relationship in my life, but I don't have to have one]…and if I don't, then I'm still somebody.'

Third, in other forms of sociotropic sadness (which I call 'discomfort-related sociotropic sadness'), the person is able to bear the resultant conditions that exist following their loss. For example:

- '[I want to be liked, but I don't have to be liked]…and if I'm not, I can bear it, it's worth doing so and I am going to do so.'
- '[I want to loved, but I don't have to be]…and if I'm not, it's bad, but not awful.'
- '[I want to be connected to people that I care about, but I don't have to be]…and if I'm not, then that would be a challenge but I would not disintegrate as I am strong enough to look after myself.'
- '[I want to have a special relationship in my life, but I don't have to have one]…and if I don't, my life still has much potential without such a relationship.'

Focusing on sociotropic loss only when it has occurred

If a person holds general flexible/non-extreme attitudes towards loss with respect to being liked, loved, etc. and these are triggered in some way, they will only tend to lead the person to focus on such loss if the loss has happened in the present. They will not tend to access past losses or think about potential future losses.

Bringing a specific flexible/non-extreme attitude to a specific sociotropic loss

When a person has experienced a specific sociotropic loss, the person brings a specific flexible/non-extreme to this loss. For example, Harriet's friend Georgia clearly rejected her and Harriet brought a specific flexible/non-extreme attitude to this rejection and felt sad ('I would have preferred it if Georgia had not rejected me, but that does not mean that it absolutely should not have happened; it did and I can still accept myself').

The effects of flexible/non-extreme attitudes towards sociotropic loss on behaviour

When a person feels sociotropically sad, the flexible/non-extreme attitudes that underpin this sadness impact on their behaviour. They seek reinforcements after a period of mourning their loss, create an environment consistent with sad feelings, express their feelings about loss in a non-complaining way to others and allow themselves to be comforted in a way that enables them to express their feelings. In short, their behaviour tends to be constructive.

The effects of flexible/non-extreme attitudes towards sociotropic loss on subsequent thinking

One important effect of sadness-related flexible/non-extreme attitudes is on a person's subsequent thinking. When a person experiences sadness, they are able to recognise negative and positive aspects of the loss that they experienced, and they think that they are able to help themself and can look to the future with hope. In other words, their thinking is realistic, balanced and non-ruminative.

Metaphors and images in sociotropic sadness

When a person experiences sociotropic sadness, they will tend to create images or metaphors that illustrate how they feel. Here are some examples of such images and metaphors that depict sociotropic sadness:

- 'I am sad, but remain connected to others in solitary isolation with no way out.'
- 'I see others enjoying themselves and I can see myself joining in once I have mourned my loss.'
- 'I see myself sad but with loving people around me.'

Autonomous sadness

As I pointed out earlier in this chapter, there are two types of sadness: sociotropic sadness and autonomous sadness. If you recall, in sociotropic sadness the person is sad about issues such as loss of affiliation, loss of love, loss of being connected to people and loss of relationships, whereas in autonomous sadness the person is sad about losses of freedom, autonomy, competence and status. In this section, I will discuss autonomous sadness.

The role of general flexible/non-extreme attitudes in autonomous sadness

When a person experiences autonomous sadness, they tend to hold a number of general flexible/non-extreme attitudes.

First, they tend to hold a *flexible attitude* towards the place of achieving key goals and standards in their life such as achievement, being competent, self-reliant, autonomous and having high status. In the following list, I will once again provide both the preference component and the negated demand component of a flexible attitude. The attitudes in round brackets show how each attitude is commonly expressed in everyday life.

- 'I want to achieve important goals in life, but I don't have to achieve them.' ('I don't have to achieve important life goals.')
- 'I want to be competent, but I don't have to be so.' ('I don't have to be competent.')
- 'I want to be able to determine my life path free from external restrictions, but I don't have to do so.' ('I don't have to be able to determine my life path free from external restrictions.')
- 'I want to be self-reliant, but I don't have to be so.' ('I don't have to be self-reliant.')
- 'I want to achieve a set status in life and therefore I have to do so.' ('I must achieve a set status in life.')

Second, in some forms of autonomous sadness, the person tends to hold an *unconditional self-acceptance attitude* towards these issues. I call this type of depression 'self-acceptance autonomous sadness' because the person does not base self-esteem on the presence of conditions such as achievement, competence, self-reliance, autonomy and status. In the following examples, I show the flexible attitudes in square brackets and then list the unconditional self-acceptance attitudes that stem from these fluid ideas:

- '[I want to achieve what I want in life, but I don't have to do so]…and if I don't, I am not a failure. I am a fallible human being capable of succeeding and failing.'
- '[I want to be competent, but I don't have to be so]…and if I'm not, I am not an idiot. I am an ordinary human being capable of doing well and poorly.'
- '[I want to be able to determine my life path free from external restrictions, but I don't have to do so']…and if I can't, then I am still a fallible human who can determine what I can control. I am not useless.'
- '[I want to be self-reliant, but I don't have to be so]…and if I'm not, then I am not a weak person. I am a person with strengths and weaknesses.'
- '[I want to achieve the status in life that I set for myself, but I don't have to do so]…and if I don't, then I am not worthless. I'm a fallible human whose worth is not determined by my status.'

Third, in other forms of autonomous sadness (which I call 'discomfort-related autonomous sadness'), the person is able to bear the resultant conditions that exist following their loss. For example:

- '[I want to achieve what I want in life, but I don't have to do so]... and if I don't, I can bear it. It's worth bearing and I am both willing to do so and I am going to do so.'
- '[I want to be competent, but I don't have to be so]...and if I'm not, it's bad, but not awful.'
- '[I want to be able to determine my life path free from external restrictions, but I don't have to do so']...and if I am not able to, it's difficult, but bearable. It's worth it to bear these restrictions and I am both willing to do so and I am going to do so.'
- '[I want to be self-reliant, but I don't have to be so]...and it's bad, but not the end of the world if I'm not.'
- '[I want to achieve the status in life that I set for myself, but I don't have to do so]...and if I don't, it would be a struggle for me to bear it, but I could do so and I am determined to do so.'

Focusing on autonomous loss

If a person holds general flexible/non-extreme attitudes towards loss with respect to failing, being constrained, losing status, etc. and these are triggered in some way, they will only tend to lead the person to focus on such loss if the loss has happened in the present. They will not tend to access past losses or think about potential future losses.

Bringing a specific flexible/non-extreme attitude to a specific autonomous loss

When a person has experienced a specific autonomous loss, the person brings a specific flexible/non-extreme to this loss. For example, Kevin lost his job and brought a specific flexible/non-extreme attitude to this loss and felt sad ('I would have preferred it if I had not lost my job, but that does not mean that it absolutely should not have happened. It did and I can still accept myself. I am not a failure.')

The effects of flexible/non-extreme attitudes towards autonomous loss on behaviour

When a person feels autonomously sad, the flexible/non-extreme attitudes that underpin this sadness impact on their behaviour. Their

64 Depression and sadness

actions here are similar to how a person acts when they hold flexible/non-extreme attitudes towards a sociotropic loss (see above). In other words, these behaviours tend to be constructive.

The effects of flexible/non-extreme attitudes towards autonomous loss on subsequent thinking

When a person experiences autonomous sadness, their flexible/non-extreme attitudes influence their subsequent thinking in that it becomes realistic, balanced and non-ruminative. Their thoughts here are similar to how a person thinks when they hold flexible/non-extreme attitudes towards a sociotropic loss (see above).

Metaphors and images in autonomous sadness

When a person is in an autonomously sad frame of mind, they will tend to create images or metaphors that illustrate how they feel. Here are some examples of such images and metaphors that depict autonomous depression:

- 'My life is full of failure and success.'
- 'I see others and myself succeeding and reaching our goals, even though I am struggling to reach mine at the moment.'
- 'I pull my own strings even though I may not be able to be in full control.'
- 'I see myself looking after myself even if others have to help me.'

Plight pity

In Chapter 3, I discussed self- and other-pity which are key components in some forms of depression. The healthy alternative to this is what I call plight pity, which the person experiences without self-pity and other-pity. Plight pity occurs where the person feels sorry that they or others are experiencing a bad situation but where they do not feel sorry for themself or for others.

Plight pity without self-pity

When a person feels sorry for the plight that they are in, but does not feel self-pity, the following tends to happen:

1   The person tends to focus on an aspect of their life where they consider that they have been treated badly or where they have failed to achieve something that they have worked very hard for. In particular, this aspect may be one where the person clearly thinks that (a) they did not deserve the bad treatment and (b) they deserved to achieve what they were striving for. In addition, the person is more likely to experience plight pity where others involved were unfairly advantaged.
2   The person tends to bring the following flexible/non-extreme attitude to these inferences at A (which may or may not be accurate):
    • 'I would much prefer not to be treated badly when I don't deserve to be (and when others are unfairly advantaged), but sadly the world, in this respect, does not have to be what I want it to be and when this occurs (a) it's bad but not terrible and (b) the world is a complex mixture of the good, the bad and the neutral and is not a rotten place for allowing this to happen to me. I am not a person to be pitied, but a non-pitiable person who is in a pitiable situation.'
    • 'When I work hard for something, it would be highly desirable for me to get what I think I deserve (particularly when others are unfairly advantaged), but it does not have to be the way I want it to be. When I don't get what I think I deserve, (a) it's bad but not terrible and (b) the world is a complex mixture of the good, the bad and the neutral and is not a rotten place for allowing this to happen to me. I am not a person to be pitied, but a non-pitiable person who is in a pitiable situation.'
3   These flexible/non-extreme attitudes tend to influence the person's subsequent thinking. As I have already shown in this book, once a person brings a flexible/non-extreme attitude to a threat to or a loss from their personal domain, then this attitude influences their subsequent thinking in realistic and balanced ways.

    Thus, when a person thinks that they have undeservedly been treated badly and they hold a flexible/non-extreme attitude towards this as shown in (a) above, then they will tend to:
    • Think in a balanced way about previous occasions where they have been treated badly when they have not merited such treatment and where they have been treated well and deservedly.
    • Focus on both the unfairnesses that they have suffered and the unfairnesses that have been in their favour.

When the person has worked hard for something and hasn't been awarded it and others less deserving of the award have received it, and they hold a flexible/non-extreme attitude towards this as detailed in (b) above, then they will tend to:
- Think about other occasions when their hard work failed to be rewarded as well as occasions when they have been rewarded for working hard and occasions when they were rewarded for not working particularly hard.
- Think about occasions when others have been rewarded for not working particularly hard and about occasions when their hard labours or efforts have also not been rewarded.

4 The person does not tend to complain to others about their poor plight, but when they do, they speak in a balanced way about it.

Plight pity without other-pity

When a person feels sorry for the plight of others but not for them as people, the following tends to happen:

1 The person focuses on an aspect of life where they consider that other people are being treated very badly through no fault of their own.
2 The person tends to bring the following flexible/non-extreme attitude to these inferences at *A* (which may or may not be accurate):
- 'It would be highly desirable if the world were not to allow such bad treatment to happen; however, sadly and regretfully, the world does not have to be such a place. The world is a place where a multitude of good, bad and neutral things happen. It is very bad for such treatment to be meted out to the person (or people), but it is not the end of the world. These people are in a poor plight, but they are not pitiable people.'
3 This flexible/non-extreme attitude tends to influence the person's subsequent thinking. Thus, when they think that others have been treated badly through no fault of their own and the person holds a flexible/non-extreme attitude towards this (as shown above), then they will tend to:
- Focus on both the unfairnesses and bad treatment that innocent 'victims' have had to endure as well as all the fairnesses

that others have benefited from. In short, the person focuses on both man's inhumanity to man and man's humanity to man.
- Think that the world is not getting worse in this respect and that there is still hope for humankind.

4   The person does not tend to complain to others about the poor plight of others, but when they do, they speak in a balanced way about it.

Sadness about depression

I mentioned earlier in the book that, as humans, we have the ability not only to disturb ourselves, but to disturb ourselves about our disturbances. However, we can also not disturb ourselves about our disturbances, and in this part of the chapter I will discuss how a person can feel sad but not depressed about depression.

How a person can feel sad but not depressed about the physical aspects of depression

As I mentioned in Chapter 3, depression can be physically painful. A person may, for example, have difficulty sleeping, may lose their appetite and may have physical aches and pains.

When a person feels sad but not depressed about the physical aspects of their depression, they tend to:

- Focus on the physical aspects of their depression.
- Bring the following flexible/non-extreme attitude to these aspects: 'I would prefer not to feel so bad, but it does not have to be the way I want it to be. It is a struggle for me to put up with these feelings, but I can do so. It is worth it to me to bear these feelings, I am willing to and I am going to do so.'
- Engage in the behavioural and thinking consequences of this attitude:
  Behavioural consequence: Become active and engage in enjoyable activities. This will have the effect of having the person focus away from the physical pain of their depression.
  Thinking consequence: 'I will get over this pain. It is likely to be time-limited.'

Unconditional self-acceptance about depression

A person can accept themself unconditionally about depressing themself in the first place in a number of ways. I will group these ways together.

- The person focuses on what being depressed means for them, e.g. a weakness, a failing, evidence of having an unlovable trait.
- They then bring to this inference one of the following flexible/non-extreme attitudes and engage in the illustrative behavioural and thinking consequences of this attitude.

> 'I would prefer to not be weak (by being depressed), but that does not mean that I must not have such a weakness. I am not a weak person for having this weakness. I am a fallible human being who has strengths and weaknesses.'
> *Behavioural consequence*: Faces up to people.
> *Thinking consequence*: Rethinks whether depression is a weakness or not and is likely to think that it isn't.

> 'Being depressed means that I am failing and while I would prefer not to fail, there is no law that stipulates that I must not do so. I am not a failure but a fallible human being capable of succeeding and failing.'
> *Behavioural consequence*: Still try even if there is a chance of failing.
> *Thinking consequence*: Rethinks whether depression is a failing or not and is likely to think that it isn't.

> 'Being depressed demonstrates that I have an unlovable trait that I would prefer not to have, but it does not mean that I must not have it. Because I have, it does not prove that I am an unlovable person. It proves that I am an ordinary person with lovable and unlovable features.'
> *Behavioural consequence*: Relates to loved ones when depressed without trying to put on a brave face.
> *Thinking consequence*: Rethinks whether depression is an unlovable trait and is likely to think that it isn't.

It is important to note that when a person thinks that depression is a weakness, a failing or an unlovable trait and devalues themself, they first need to develop an unconditional self-acceptance attitude towards one or more of these features before reconsidering whether depression is representative of such features.

People develop and rehearse a view of the world founded on sadness-related flexible/non-extreme attitudes

I mentioned in the previous chapter that people develop world views that render them vulnerable or protect them from particular unhealthy negative emotions. The world views that render a person liable to experience sadness are as follows, together with the inferences that they spawn.

World view: Life has meaning but can seem meaningless at times.
Inference: I can pursue things that have meaning for me, but at times I may lose my way when I have experienced a significant loss, for example.

World view: Some people may ultimately reject me, but others will ultimately accept me.
Inference: If people get to know the real me, some will accept me and some will reject me.

World view: There are no strong and weak people, only people with strengths and weaknesses.
Inference: I can be strong and independent and weak and dependent.

Maintaining sadness in the face of loss

When a person feels sad, but not depressed, they need to do the following to maintain sadness and protect themselves from depression:

- They get up and wash and make sure they get exercise.
- They read good and bad news stories in daily newspapers.
- They play music that reflects sadness and refrain from playing the 'music of misery'.
- They may withdraw temporarily from events that they are likely to enjoy, but they come back to such events after a period of mourning and healthy processing of their loss.

- They will keep doing things that are important to them whether they fail or succeed. They learn from failure without self-devaluation and take credit for being successful.

In the next part of the book, I will discuss shame and its healthy alternative, disappointment.

Part 3

Shame and disappointment

Chapter 5

Understanding shame

Shame and guilt are often linked together in people's minds and are often seen as similar emotions. While there are certain similarities to these two emotions, they also have important differences and as such they warrant a chapter each. Consequently, I will show you how a person makes themself feel ashamed in this chapter and feel guilty in Chapter 7. In the next chapter, I will discuss the emotion of disappointment, the healthy alternative to shame.

The components of shame

In order for a person to feel ashamed and maintain these feelings, they tend to do the following:

1. They make certain types of inference.
2. They bring shame-based rigid/extreme attitudes to those inferences.
3. They think in ways that are consistent with the above rigid/extreme attitudes.
4. They act in ways that are consistent with these rigid/extreme attitudes.
5. They rehearse a general version of their specific shame-based rigid/extreme attitudes so that they routinely make shame-based inferences about what is generally going on in their life.
6. They develop and rehearse a shame-based world view.

So let me deal with these issues one at a time.

Inferences in shame

In order to feel ashamed, a person needs to make one or more inferences about what is going on in their life. It is important to note that these inferences do not have to reflect accurately what is happening or what has happened. The important point is that the person has to believe that they are true. Here is a list of common inferences in shame:

'I've fallen short of my ideal'

When a person feels ashamed, they focus on some aspect of their life where they consider that they have fallen short (often very short) of their ideal, particularly in relation to some social code. Shame is often experienced when others are physically present, but if they are not, then the person can still feel ashamed if they imagine that they are present or that they have discovered what they did (or did not do).

People who feel ashamed do so because they infer that they have fallen short in their behaviour, in what they think or imagine, in what they feel, or in some aspect of their physical self. Let me unpack and exemplify this statement.

THE PERSON FOCUSES ON THEIR BEHAVIOUR

This could concern what the person did or what they failed to do. Here are some examples:

- They identify something they did that constitutes a weakness in their eyes (e.g. crying in public, acting foolishly in public).
- They identify an incident where they broke a social code (e.g. they spoke about a taboo topic in front of a group of people).
- They identify an incident where they failed to live up to their social code (e.g. they consider it to be important to treat people politely, but failed to treat a waiter with politeness).

THE PERSON FOCUSES ON THEIR THOUGHTS AND IMAGES

Here are some examples of thoughts and images that people feel ashamed about:

Understanding shame

- They think of harming their child.
- They picture themself having sex with an inappropriate person.
- They think 'blasphemous' thoughts.

THE PERSON FOCUSES ON THEIR EMOTIONS AND HOW THEY EXPRESS THEM

Some examples are:

- They feel unhealthily angry towards significant others.
- They show their anger in a 'nasty' way.
- They feel maliciously envious towards a friend for being pregnant.
- They demonstrate their unhealthy jealousy in public.

THE PERSON FOCUSES ON THEIR BODY

Here the person might feel ashamed of some aspect of their body that they consider to be particularly unattractive. For example:

- A nose that they consider to be too big.
- Buttocks and/or thighs that they consider to be too fat.
- A skinny frame.

'I've let down my reference group'

A reference group is a group with whom a person closely identifies. A person probably has a number of reference groups in their life, for example their family, friendship groups, their religious group and their cultural group. Each of these groups has 'let down' rules – behavioural rules that if the person breaks, the group would consider that they have let them down. As with other inferences, the inference that the person has let down a reference group may or may not be accurate.

When a person feels ashamed about letting down a reference group, then:

- They break a 'let down' rule of a valued reference group.
- They think that the group 'feels' let down by them.

Here are some examples of how a person can let down their reference group:

- Marry out of their religion.
- Get caught stealing.
- Display emotion in public.

'I've been let down by a member of my reference group'

A person may also feel ashamed when a member of their reference group has broken one of the group's 'let down' rules and then thinks that that person has let them and the group down. Typical examples are the same as those listed above, namely where the other person has:

- Married out of the person's religion.
- Got caught stealing.
- Displayed emotion in public.

'Others are judging me negatively'

It is difficult for a person to feel ashamed without making the inference that another person, but more frequently a group of people, judges them negatively. Again, whether or not these people are actually making such negative judgements is not as important as whether the person thinks they are. The person's feelings of shame are more likely to be acute if the group judging them negatively is physically present, but such feelings can also be present if they think about the group making such negative judgements.

What type of judgements does a person think others make of them when they feel ashamed? Here is a sample:

- Others communicate their displeasure at the person directly.
- Others communicate their disgust at the person directly.
- Others turn away from the person in disgust.
- Others demonstrate that they look down on the person.
- Others ignore the person.

The person holds and rehearses rigid/extreme attitudes towards their inference

If there is a main point that I want to stress in this book, it is this: at the core of emotional disturbance, the person holds a set of rigid/extreme attitudes towards the inferences that they make. In this context, a person will not feel ashamed about (a) falling short of their ideal, (b) letting down their reference group, (c) being let down by a member of their reference group and/or (d) others evaluating them negatively without holding rigid/extreme attitudes towards these inferences.

So let me discuss which rigid/extreme attitudes are at the root of shame. As you will see, they take the form of a rigid demand and a self-devaluation attitude towards the four shame-related inferences discussed above. In the following sections I will outline the general rigid/extreme attitude and illustrate it with a specific example.

Shame about falling short of an ideal

In general, in order to feel ashamed about falling short of an ideal, the person needs to hold a rigid demand about such a falling short (e.g. 'I must not fall short of my ideal') and a self-devaluation attitude towards their shortfall (e.g. '...and because I have fallen short, I am an inadequate person'). For example, Robert's ideal was to handle matters without showing anger. One day at work he lost his temper in front of his work colleagues. He felt ashamed about his shortfall by holding and practising the following shame-based rigid/extreme attitude: 'I must not lose my temper in public and because I did, I am an inadequate person.'

Shame about letting down a reference group

In general, when a person feels ashamed about letting down their reference group, they hold a rigid demand about such a letting down (e.g. 'I must not let my reference group down') and a consequent self-devaluation attitude (e.g. '...and because I have let them down, I am a shameful person'). For example, Petra belongs to a gang whose code of honour is always to support one another no matter what. Let's suppose further that Petra breaks that code by failing to support another gang member, thus letting down the gang. In order to make herself feel ashamed about her behaviour, she needs to hold and practise the following shame-based rigid/extreme attitude: 'I absolutely should not have betrayed my fellow gang member and because I did, I am a shameful person.'

Shame about being let down by a member of a reference group

When a person feels ashamed about being let down by their reference group, they hold a rigid demand about such a let down (e.g. 'A member of my reference group must not let me and the group down') and a self-devaluation attitude towards this situation (e.g. '...and because they have let us down, it proves that we are inadequate'). For example, one of Adele's reference group that she holds dear considers crying in public to be a 'let down'. One day, Fred, a member of Adele's reference group, cried in front of others; she viewed this as Fred letting her reference group down. Adele felt ashamed of Fred's 'let down' behaviour because she held the following shame-based rigid/extreme attitude: 'Fred absolutely should not have broken down in tears in front of other people and because he did, it proves that we are all (in our reference group) inadequate, weak, spineless individuals.'

Shame when being judged negatively in a shame-related context

When a person feels ashamed when others judge them negatively in a shame-related context (and again what is important here is that the person thinks that these others are judging them rather than the facts of the situation), they once again hold a rigid demand about such a negative judgement (e.g. 'Others must not judge me negatively') and a self-devaluation attitude towards this judgement (e.g. '...and because they have judged me negatively, it proves that I am inadequate'). For example, Michael spoke up in a social context and mentioned something that was a taboo in that group. Michael thought that those present turned away from him in disgust. He felt ashamed about this negative judgement because he held the following shame-based rigid/extreme attitude: 'This group absolutely should not have turned away from me in disgust and because they did, it proves that I am inadequate.'

The major negative self-judgements in shame

I have made it clear in this section that at the core of shame a person holds shame-based rigid/extreme attitudes. I have stressed that these rigid/extreme attitudes have two major components: a rigid demand and a self-devaluation attitude. A rigid demand is straightforward. It is absolute and comes in the form of a 'must', 'absolutely should', 'have to', 'got to', amongst others. Self-devaluation attitudes in shame are more varied, and in this section I will outline the major shame-based negative self-judgements. Before I list these self-devaluation attitudes, it is worth remembering that a self-devaluation attitude involves a person making a global negative judgement about their entire self. The person is not just rating a part of themselves, they are rating the whole of themself.

'I am defective'

People who feel ashamed often say: 'There is something wrong with me.' They don't mean that they are a fallible human being who may be defective in some respect. Rather, they mean that they are defective as a whole. In expressing this view, one of my clients said: 'If I was a car, the garage would say that I was beyond repair and should be scrapped.' In this context, when a person feels ashamed, they focus on an aspect of themselves that is negative and could do with improvement and then overgeneralise from this to the whole of their 'self'. In essence, the person holds the attitude: 'Because this part of me is defective, then I am defective.' As you will see, this process of overgeneralising from a part of oneself to the whole of oneself is common to all shame-based negative self-judgements.

'I am insignificant'

Sometimes when people feel ashamed, they say that they 'feel small'. Behind this 'feeling' is the self-devaluation attitude 'I am insignificant' and if a person holds this attitude, it is often in response to a situation where they have inferred, rightly or wrongly, that another person has belittled them in public. Here the person judges themself in the same way as they think the other person has judged them. It is as if the person thinks: 'I am who I think you say I am.'

'I am not good enough'

As I have already stated, people often feel ashamed when they fall short of their ideal. As I noted when discussing the 'I am defective' shame-based self-devaluation attitude, people experiencing shame often make the part–whole error. This is also true when the content of the self-devaluation attitude is 'I am not good enough'. Here they begin by noting that they have failed to measure up to some ideal in some way. In this *part* of their life, the person may be correct in saying that they are not good enough *in this* respect, meaning that they have not yet reached a certain standard. Then they make a logical error in overgeneralising from that aspect to their entire self.

For example: 'Because I am not good enough at public speaking, I am not good enough as a person.'

'I am weak/pathetic'

Listening to the self-evaluations that people who experience much shame in their lives make reveals that they often refer to themselves as being weak or pathetic. Thus, one of the ideals that such people demand that they must achieve is some sort of 'strength', either physical or mental. The latter particularly is prominent in shame. Thus, when a person feels ashamed in this area, they focus on some aspect of their life where they are not as strong as they believe they absolutely should be. Then they globally rate themself as weak or pathetic. For example, Norma considers that it is weak to cry in public. One day, she cried in front of other people and felt ashamed about doing so. She felt ashamed about this weak display because she held the following rigid/extreme attitude: 'I must not cry in public and because I did, I am a pathetic weak person.'

'I am disgusting'

The final way that a person can make themself feel ashamed is to view themself as a disgusting person. A frequent focus for a person's self-disgust is their body. For example, Christina had what she considered to be fat thighs. She made herself ashamed about her thighs by first making the following demand, 'My thighs absolutely should not be fat', and by then rating herself as disgusting: 'Because my thighs look disgusting, I am disgusting.' A person can apply this process to any aspect of their body that they particularly dislike.

How a person can make themself feel ashamed by evaluating themself according to what happened to them

When a person feels ashamed about what has happened to them, they first demand that what happened absolutely should not have happened to them and then they overgeneralise the negative rating that they make of the event to their entire self. Thus, Ruth was ridiculed in public by an acquaintance. She believed first that this absolutely should not have happened to her and then told herself that this ridicule proves that she is a stupid, shameful person.

Unconditional shame

So far, I have discussed the situation where a person makes themself conditionally ashamed, which means that they feel ashamed when they hold rigid/extreme attitudes towards:

- Falling short of their ideal.
- Letting down their reference group.
- Being let down by a member of their reference group.
- Being evaluated negatively by others.

Some people, however, think they are insignificant, defective or disgusting etc. because they are alive or because of who they are. In other words, their shame is unconditional. Consequently, it is unremitting and ever present.

Thinking that stems from shame-based rigid/extreme attitudes

When a person holds a shame-based rigid/extreme attitude towards thinking that (a) they have fallen very short of their ideal, (b) they have let down their reference group, (c) they have been let down by a member of their reference group and (d) others are judging them negatively, this attitude will influence the way that they subsequently think. This thinking is characterised by exaggeration, overestimation of negative consequences and failure to appreciate that there may be a variety of responses to one's behaviour.

For example, Theo made himself feel ashamed about saying something stupid in front of a group of people. The shame-based thinking consequences of his rigid/extreme attitudes were as follows.

Overestimating the 'shamefulness' of one's behaviour

Theo thought that what he said was very stupid (rather than moderately or mildly stupid).

Overestimating the extent to which others will notice one's 'shameful' behaviour

Theo thought that everyone present took notice of what he said.

Overestimating the likelihood that others will regard one's behaviour as 'shameful'

Theo thought that it was highly likely that everyone present thought that what he said was stupid.

Overestimating the extent to which others will regard one's behaviour as 'shameful'

Theo thought that those present regarded his behaviour as very stupid (rather than moderately or mildly stupid).

Overestimating the length of time that others will remember one's 'shameful' behaviour

Theo thought that those present would remember what he said for a very long time.

Overestimating the likelihood that others will regard one as 'shameful'

Theo thought that it was highly likely that those present considered that he (rather than just his behaviour) was stupid.

Overestimating the extent to which others will regard one as 'shameful'

Theo thought that those present regarded him as very stupid (rather than mildly or moderately stupid).

Overestimating the length of time that others will regard one as 'shameful'

Theo thought that those present would consider him stupid for a very long time.

Overestimating the likelihood that those observing will tell others about one

Theo thought that it was highly likely that those present would tell others about what he said.

Understanding shame

Exaggerating what those observing will tell others about one

Theo thought that those present would tell others what a very stupid person he was.

Exaggerating the extent to which others will ridicule one

Theo thought that those present would ridicule him very badly.

Exaggerating the extent to which others will exclude one

Theo thought that those present would exclude him and not want anything to do with him in the future.

It is important to bear in mind that while all the above thinking consequences of shame-based rigid/extreme attitudes are possible, the extent to which they are likely to occur is grossly exaggerated by the person.

Behaviour that stems from shame-based rigid/extreme attitudes

When a person holds shame-based rigid/extreme attitudes, they will tend to act in certain ways. Many of these behaviours are both an expression of shame and an attempt by the person to avoid the pain of these feelings and/or the adversity at A. The main point to note is that these behaviours both stem from the person's shame-based rigid/extreme attitudes and, when they engage in them, help to strengthen their conviction in these attitudes. As such, engaging in the following shame-based behaviours renders the person more vulnerable to experiencing shame.

Physically withdrawing from others

When a person feels ashamed, they will experience a strong tendency to physically withdraw from the people they think have witnessed their 'shameful' behaviour and are evaluating them negatively for it. When the person gives in to this tendency and actually withdraws from these people, they will immediately experience a sense of relief. However, this will be short-lived and withdrawing in this way will result in the person experiencing shame in the future because they have strengthened their shame-based rigid/extreme attitudes. By physically withdrawing from others after revealing a weakness to them, for example, the person is in effect saying: 'If I remain in the presence of these people after acting weakly in front of them, I will see them look down on me and this will mean that I am a weak person for acting weakly, which I absolutely should not have done. Therefore I will leave.'

Looking away from others

When a person experiences shame in the presence of others, they will tend to look down and away from the gaze of these other people. Doing so will result in the person unwittingly strengthening their shame-based rigid/extreme attitudes. Averting their gaze from others is a form of psychological withdrawal. It strengthens shame-based rigid/extreme attitudes in a way similar to physically withdrawing from others. By looking away from others, after revealing a weakness to them, for example, the person is in effect saying: 'If I look at these people after acting weakly in front of them, I will see them look down on me and this will mean that I am a weak person for acting weakly, which I absolutely should not have done. Therefore I will avoid their gaze.'

Isolating oneself from others

Once a person feels ashamed and perhaps after they have physically withdrawn from the shame-related situation, they will tend to perpetuate their shame-based rigid/extreme attitude by isolating themself from others. For example, when Christina did this, she was in effect saying: 'Because I am a disgusting person for revealing my fat thighs in public, I'll avoid other people in case they see them.'

Denying responsibility for one's actions

When a person has made themself feel ashamed, they will be tempted to get rid of these feelings of shame by denying responsibility for their actions. Once again, doing so will perpetuate their shame-based rigid/extreme attitudes and make it more likely that they will feel shame in the future. Let me give you an example. Sandra insulted her boss's husband at the works Christmas party. She began to feel ashamed because she believed that she showed herself to be stupid. To get rid of these feelings, she quickly denied responsibility for her actions by blaming them on the medication that she claimed to be taking (but in reality wasn't).

Concealing verbally and physically

Shame and concealment often go together. A person can hide when they feel ashamed and they can hide in order to prevent themself from feeling ashamed. Either way, when a person acts in a concealing manner, they reinforce their shame-based rigid/extreme attitudes.

When a person uses verbal concealment, they decide to say very little about themself to others. They tend to be quite superficial in their conversations with others and certainly do not say anything that might be taken as controversial by those present. The reason why the person conceals is to avoid feeling ashamed. It is as if they are saying to themself: 'I will not reveal anything that could be construed as controversial about myself because if I do, others may look down on me and I must not be disapproved by others. If this happens, it proves that I am inadequate.'

When concealment is physical, the person hides aspects of their body from others because they feel ashamed of themself for having such aspects. For example, Christina's concealment of her thighs was underpinned by a shame-creating rigid/extreme attitude: 'Others must not see how fat my thighs are, and if they do, they will think that I am disgusting and they would be right. I am disgusting for having my fat thighs. Therefore, I will hide them from public view.'

Overcompensating for one's feelings of shame

Another way in which a person unwittingly perpetuates their shame-creating rigid/extreme attitudes, and thus makes it more likely that they feel shame, is for that person to act in a way that overcompensates for their shame. For example, Warren, who feels ashamed of being small and of weak stature, overcompensates for this by showing everyone how physically strong he is.

Thus, when a person overcompensates for their feelings of shame, they tend to do the very opposite of what they feel ashamed about.

People develop and rehearse general shame-based rigid/extreme attitudes

General shame-based rigid/extreme attitudes are rigid/extreme attitudes that a person holds in many theme-related situations that result in them experiencing shame in these situations. Developing and rehearsing such attitudes will lead the person to experience shame in many different situations. They will do this mainly because they become skilled at inferring, for example, that they have fallen short of their ideal and that other people will evaluate them negatively for this even when there is scant supporting evidence for the latter.

Let me show you how this works. First, the person develops general shame-based rigid/extreme attitudes, such as 'I must always live up to my ideals and if I don't, then I am inadequate' and 'Other people must not disapprove of me and if they do, it proves that I am inadequate'. They then rehearse these attitudes until they have strong conviction in them and bring them to relevant situations where it is possible that (a) they will not live up to their ideals and (b) others will disapprove of them. Then, because the person cannot convince themself that they will live up to their ideals and that they will not be disapproved of, they think that they have fallen short of their ideals (in a big way) and that people will disapprove of them for this. Having created these shame-based inferences, they develop and hold specific versions of these general shame-based rigid/extreme attitudes towards these inferences and thereby make themself feel ashamed in these specific situations.

Let me give you a concrete example. Stephen developed the following two general shame-based rigid/extreme attitudes: 'I must never lose my temper in public and if I do, I am a weak person' and 'Others must approve of me and if they don't, I am inadequate'. He took these two attitudes to a specific situation where a waiter in a restaurant brought him the wrong dish and he snapped at the waiter very briefly. Stephen's two general shame-based rigid/extreme attitudes led him to make the following inferences about this event: (a) 'I lost my temper with the waiter' (because of his first general shame-based rigid/extreme attitude he inferred that snapping briefly at the waiter was tantamount to losing his temper with him) and (b) 'Others witnessing this disapproved of me for losing my temper with the waiter' (because of his second general shame-based rigid/extreme attitude he inferred that because those present would not approve of him for this incident, therefore they would disapprove of him for it). Stephen's attitude did not permit him to consider that they might think he was justified in his behaviour or that they did not take any notice or that they might briefly disapprove of his behaviour but still basically approve of him.

Once Stephen created his inferences, he made himself feel ashamed about them by holding specific versions of his general shame-inducing rigid/extreme attitudes: 'I lost my temper with the waiter and incurred the disapproval of those present. I absolutely should not have done either of these things and because I did, I am a weak, inadequate person.'

Then, Stephen thought and acted in ways that were consistent with his shame-based rigid/extreme attitudes, which had the effect of strengthening his conviction in these attitudes.

People develop and rehearse a view of the world founded on shame-based rigid/extreme attitudes

I have said that people develop ideas about the world as it relates to them and some of these 'world views' render them vulnerable to particular unhealthy negative emotions. The world views that render a person vulnerable to shame do so because they make it very easy for them to make shame-related inferences. Then, as I have shown earlier in the chapter, the person makes themselves feel ashamed about these inferences with the appropriate rigid/extreme attitudes. Here is an illustrative list of shame-related world views that a person may develop and the inferences that they spawn.

World view: There is always the danger that I will not achieve my ideal standards.
Inference: I have not reached my ideal and am showing a weakness.

World view: Social situations are dangerous because I may be exposed at any moment.
Inference: If I reveal a weakness, no matter how small, people will easily spot this.

World view: Social situations are dangerous because other people will judge me negatively if I put a foot wrong.
Inference: If I reveal a weakness, people will judge me negatively.

In the next chapter, I will consider the emotion of disappointment, which I consider to be the healthy alternative to shame.

Further reading

Academic

Tangney, J.P. & Dearing, R.L. (2002). *Shame and guilt.* New York: Guilford.

Self-help

Dryden, W. (1997). *Overcoming shame.* London: Sheldon.

Chapter 6

Understanding disappointment

In Chapter 2 I argued that concern is the healthy emotion alternative to anxiety and in Chapter 4 I made the case that sadness is the healthy emotion alternative to depression. In this chapter, I will argue that disappointment is the healthy emotion alternative to shame. While the components of disappointment are clear, the term 'disappointment' has not been universally accepted as a plausible name for this emotion. Some argue that we should use the terms 'unhealthy shame' and 'healthy shame' to distinguish between the two emotions and I have sympathy with this view (and use this convention myself later to distinguish between the unhealthy and healthy forms of anger, jealousy and envy). However, in this chapter I will use the term disappointment to denote the healthy alternative to shame.

The components of disappointment

When a person feels disappointment:

1 They make certain types of inference.
2 They bring disappointment-based flexible/non-extreme attitudes to those inferences.
3 They think in ways that are consistent with the above flexible/non-extreme attitudes.
4 They act in ways that are consistent with these flexible/non-extreme attitudes.
5 They use a general version of their specific disappointment-based flexible/non-extreme attitudes which helps them to see the world more objectively than when they utilise and rehearse general shame-based rigid and extreme attitudes.
6 They develop and rehearse a disappointment-based world view.

DOI: 10.4324/9781003203483-9

Inferences in disappointment

When a person experiences disappointment as a healthy alternative to shame, they make the same inferences as they do when they experience shame. Again these inferences do not have to reflect accurately what is happening or what has happened. The important point is that the person has to believe that they are true. Here is a reminder of a list of these inferences.[1]

- 'I've fallen short of my ideal.'
- 'I've let down my reference group.'
- 'I've been let down by a member of my reference group.'
- 'Others are judging me negatively.'

The person holds and rehearses flexible/non-extreme attitudes towards one or more of the above inferences

If there is a main point that I want to stress in this book, it is this: at the core of healthy negative emotions, which are the healthy alternatives to emotional disturbance, the person holds a set of flexible/non-extreme attitudes towards the inferences that they make. In this context, a person will feel disappointed about (a) falling short of their ideal, (b) letting down their reference group, (c) being let down by a member of their reference group and/or (d) others evaluating them negatively when they hold flexible/non-extreme attitudes towards these inferences.

So let me discuss which flexible/non-extreme attitudes are at the root of disappointment. As you will see, they take the form of a flexible attitude and an unconditional self-acceptance attitude towards the four inferences listed above and discussed in Chapter 5. In the following sections I will outline the general flexible/non-extreme attitude and illustrate it with a specific example.

Disappointment about falling short of an ideal

In general, in order to feel disappointment about falling short of an ideal, the person needs to hold a flexible attitude towards such a falling short (e.g. 'I don't want to fall short of my ideal, but that does not mean that this must not happen') and an unconditional self-acceptance attitude towards their shortfall (e.g. '...and because I have fallen short, I am a fallible human being with adequacies and inadequacies. I am not an inadequate person.'). You will remember Robert, whom we first met in Chapter 5. Robert's ideal was to handle matters without showing anger. One day at work he lost his temper in front of his work colleagues. If he were to feel disappointed rather than ashamed about his shortfall, he would have had to hold and practise the following disappointment-based flexible/non-extreme attitude: 'I would much prefer not to lose my temper in public, but I am not immune from doing so and neither do I have to be so immune. Because I did lose my temper, I am a fallible human being with relative and not absolute control over my temper. I am not an inadequate person.'

Disappointment about letting down a reference group

In general, when a person feels disappointed but not ashamed about letting down their reference group, they hold a flexible attitude towards such a letting down (e.g. 'I don't want to let my reference group down, but that does not mean that I absolutely should not have done so') and a consequent unconditional self-acceptance attitude (e.g. '...and because I have let them down, it's bad that I did so, but I am not a shameful person. I'm a complex, fallible human being.'). For example, if you recall, Petra, whom we met in Chapter 5, belongs to a gang whose code of honour is always to support one another no matter what. Let's suppose further that Petra breaks that code by failing to support another gang member, thus letting down the gang. In order to feel disappointed and not ashamed about her behaviour, she needs to hold and practise the following disappointment-based flexible/non-extreme attitude: 'I really wish I had not betrayed my fellow gang member, but that does not mean that I absolutely should not have done so. Failing to support my fellow gang member does not make me a shameful person. I am an ordinary human being capable of living up to the gang's code and breaking it.'

Disappointment about being let down by a member of a reference group

When a person feels disappointed but not ashamed about being let down by their reference group, they hold a flexible attitude towards such a let down (e.g. 'I would much prefer it if a member of my reference group did not let me and the group down, but that does not mean that they must not do so') and an unconditional self-acceptance attitude towards this situation (e.g. '...and because they have let us down, it does not prove that we are inadequate. It proves that we are all human and cannot be defned by the behaviour of one of us.'). For example, one of Adele's[2] reference group (that she holds dear) considers crying in public to be a 'let down'. One day Fred, a member of Adele's reference group, cried in front of others: she viewed this as Fred letting her reference group down. Adele felt disappointed but not ashamed about Fred's 'let down' behaviour because she held the following disppointment-based flexible/non-extreme attitude: 'It would have been better if Fred had not broken down in tears in front of other people, but that does not mean that he must not do so. Fred doing so does not change the fact that we are all (in our reference group) human beings with our good points and foibles rather than inadequate, weak, spineless individuals.'

Disappointment when being judged negatively by others

When a person feels disappointment but not ashamed when others judge them negatively (and again what is important here is that the person thinks that these others are judging them rather than the facts of the situation), they once again hold a flexible attitude towards such a negative judgement (e.g. 'I don't want others to judge me negatively, but that does not mean that they must not do so') and an unconditional self-acceptance attitude towards this judgement (e.g. '...and because they have judged me negatively, it does not prove that I am inadequate. I am the same fallible human being if they judge me negatively or positively.'). For example, Michael (whom we first met in the previous chapter) spoke up in a social context and mentioned something that was a taboo in that group. Michael thought that those present turned away from him in disgust. If he felt disappointment but not ashamed about this negative judgement, he would have had to have held the following disappointment-based flexible/non-extreme attitude: 'I would have much preferred it if the group did not turn away from me in disgust, but it does not follow that they absolutely should not have done so. Their reaction does not prove that I am inadequate. I am an ordinary fallible person who did the wrong thing.'

The major attitude towards self in disappointment

I have made it clear in this section that at the core of disappointment a person holds disappointment-based flexible/non-extreme attitudes. I have stressed that these flexible/non-extreme attitudes have two major components: a flexible attitude and an unconditional self-acceptance attitude. A flexible attitude is straightforward. It is relative and comes in the form of a non-dogmatic preference involving a desire and a negated demand (e.g. 'I want to achieve my ideal, but I don't have to achieve it'). Unconditional self-acceptance attitudes in disappointment are based on a number of related ideas: that the self is complex and unrateable, fallible and fluid, and that these are the case unconditionally. This contrasts with a self-devaluation attitude in shame which involves a person making a global negative judgement about their entire self. The person is not just rating a part of themselves, they are rating the whole of themselves.

In disappointment, the person does the following:

- Acknowledges the adversity at A.
- Negates certain ideas that are present in shame:
  - 'I am not defective.'
  - 'I am not insignificant.'
  - 'I am not "not good enough".'
  - 'I am not weak/pathetic.'
  - 'I am not disgusting.'
- Asserts who they are: 'I am a complex, unrateable, unique, fluid and fallible human being.'

When a person experiences disappointment, they do not define themself according to what happened to them

When a person feels disappointment but not ashamed about what has happened to them, they first assert their preference that this did not happen to them and then negate the demand that this absolutely should not have occurred. While recognising the badness of what occurred, the person does not overgeneralise this negative rating to their entire self. Thus, Ruth, whom we met in the previous chapter, was ridiculed in public by an acquaintance. She held the flexible attitude first that it would have been much better if this hadn't happened to her, but it does not follow that it absolutely shouldn't, and then told herself that this ridicule does not define her and that she is fallible whether or not she was ridiculed.

Thinking that stems from disappointment-based flexible/non-extreme attitudes

When a person holds a disappointment-based flexible/non-extreme attitude towards thinking that (a) they have fallen very short of their ideal, (b) they have let down their reference group, (c) they have been let down by a member of their reference group and (d) others are judging them negatively, this attitude will influence the way that they subsequently think. This thinking is characterised by realism and balance, appreciating that there may be a variety of responses to one's behaviour.

For example, if Theo felt disappointed rather than ashamed about saying something stupid in front of a group of people, the disappointment-based thinking consequences of his flexible/non-extreme attitudes would have been as follows.

Being realistic about the negativity of one's behaviour

Theo thought that what he said was moderately or mildly (rather than very) stupid.

Being realistic about the extent to which others will notice one's behaviour

Theo thought that some people, but not everyone present, took notice of what he said.

Being realistic about the likelihood that others will regard one's behaviour as 'highly negative'

Theo thought that it was possible that everyone present thought that what he said was stupid, but it was more probable that some would and most wouldn't.

Being realistic about the extent to which others will regard one's behaviour as 'highly negative'

Theo thought that those present regarded his behaviour as moderately or mildly stupid (rather than very stupid).

Understanding disappointment 95

Being realistic about the length of time that others will remember one's 'negative' behaviour

Theo thought that a few of those present might remember what he said for a very long time, but that most of those who noticed it would remember it for a short time.

Being realistic about the likelihood that others will regard one as 'highly negative'

Theo thought that it was possible that some of those present considered that he (rather than just his behaviour) was stupid, but that most wouldn't.

Being realistic about the extent to which others will regard one as 'highly negative'

Theo thought that some of those present regarded him as very stupid (rather than mildly or moderately stupid), but that most of them would not regard him as stupid at all.

Being realistic about the length of time that others will regard one as 'highly negative'

Theo thought that some of those present would consider him stupid for a very long time, but that most who regarded him as stupid would do so for a short time and others would not regard him as stupid at all.

Being realistic about the likelihood that those observing will tell others about one

Theo thought that it was possible that some of those present would tell others about what he said, but that most wouldn't.

Being realistic about what those observing will tell others about one

Theo thought that maybe a few of those present would tell others what a very stupid person he was, but that most wouldn't.

Being realistic about the extent to which others will ridicule one

Theo thought that maybe one or two present would ridicule him very badly, but most wouldn't.

Being realistic about the extent to which others will exclude one

Theo thought that perhaps a few of those present would exclude him and not want anything to do with him in the future, but that most wouldn't.

It is important to bear in mind that Theo is being balanced and realistic in the thinking consequences of his disappointment-based flexible/non-extreme attitudes, recognising that the events listed are possible but unlikely, as opposed to the thinking consequences of his shame-based rigid/extreme attitudes, which are grossly exaggerated by Theo.

Behaviour that stems from disappointment-based flexible/non-extreme attitudes

When a person holds disappointment-based flexible/non-extreme attitudes, they will tend to act in certain ways. Many of these behaviours are both an expression of disappointment and a way of enabling the person to stay with the pain of these feelings. The main point to note is that these behaviours both stem from the person's disappointment-based flexible/non-extreme attitudes and, when they engage in them, help to strengthen their conviction in these attitudes. As such, engaging in the following disappointment-based behaviours renders the person more likely to experience disappointment rather than shame.

Physically staying with others

When a person feels disappointment rather than shame, they will remain physically with others even though it is uncomfortable for them to do so and even though some of these may evaluate them negatively. They can do this because they are working towards accepting themself unconditionally in the face of the adversity at *A*. Contrast this with shame, where the person experiences a strong tendency to physically withdraw from the people they think have witnessed their 'shameful' behaviour and are evaluating them negatively for it.

Looking at others

When a person experiences shame in the presence of others, they will tend to look down and away from the gaze of these other people.

However, when the person experiences disappointment rather than shame, they will be able to look at others. They will do so because they are accepting themselves unconditionally in the face of possible rejection by others.

Remaining connected with others

Once a person feels ashamed and perhaps after they have physically withdrawn from the shame-related situation, they will tend to perpetuate their shame-based rigid/extreme attitude by isolating themself from others. However, when the person experiences disappointment in the same situation, they remain connected with others because they are able to accept themselves unconditionally rather than devalue themselves.

Accepting responsibility for one's actions

When a person has made themself feel ashamed, they will be tempted to get rid of these feelings of shame by denying responsibility for their actions. This is motivated by their attitude of self-devaluation. By contrast, because disappointment is underpinned by an attitude of unconditional self-acceptance, the person is able to accept responsibility for their actions even though they may have acted in a way that falls very short of their ideal.

Being open verbally and physically

While shame and concealment often go together, when a person experiences disappointment rather than shame, they do not have to hide the fact that they are a fallible human being from themselves or from others. This leads them to be appropriately open both in what they say about themself and with respect to their physical self, even though they may not like aspects of their body.

People develop and rehearse general disappointment-based flexible/non-extreme attitudes

General disappointment-based flexible/non-extreme attitudes are attitudes that a person holds in many theme-related situations that result in them experiencing disappointment rather than shame in these situations. When they do this, they only infer that they have

98 Shame and disappointment

fallen short of their ideal and that other people will evaluate them negatively for this when it is clear that both have occurred. They will then evaluate such situations with specific variants of these general disappointment-based flexible/non-extreme attitudes.

People develop and rehearse a view of the world founded on disappointment-based flexible/non-extreme attitudes

I have made the point in previous chapters that people develop world views that render them vulnerable to or protect them from particular unhealthy negative emotions. The world views that underpin a person's tendency to experience disappointment rather than shame are as follows, together with the inferences that they spawn.

World view: While I may not always achieve my ideal standards, the main thing is that I am working towards doing so.
Inference: I have not reached my ideal, but this only means that I am showing my humanity.

World view: When I reveal that I have fallen very short of my ideal, social situations are uncomfortable but not dangerous.
Inference: If I reveal a weakness, people will only spot this when it is obvious that I have done so.

World view: When I have fallen very short of my ideal, some will judge me negatively, some won't notice and some will be compassionate towards me.
Inference: If I reveal an obvious weakness, I will get a range of responses from people.

Notes

1 See Chapter 5 for a discussion of these inferences.
2 We first met Adele in Chapter 5.

Part 4

Guilt and remorse

Chapter 7

Understanding guilt

Guilt is often linked with shame and there are certainly some similarities between the two emotions. However, there are also major differences between the two, as you will see.

Before I discuss guilt, a word on terminology. I make the distinction between being guilty and feeling guilty. By *being guilty*, I refer to the person taking responsibility for doing something wrong, for failing to do the right thing or for harming or hurting someone. By *feeling guilty*, I mean the emotion that a person experiences when they blame or condemn themself for one or more of the above. Because it is based on unhealthy rigid/extreme attitudes and generally has negative consequences, guilt is a disturbed negative emotion. A feeling of remorse is a healthy response to doing wrong, for example, because it is based on responsibility without self-blame and generally has healthy consequences. I will discuss remorse in the following chapter.

The components of guilt

In order for a person to feel guilty and stay feeling guilty, the person tends to do the following:

1. They make certain types of inference.
2. They bring guilt-based rigid/extreme attitudes to those inferences.
3. They think in ways that are consistent with the above rigid/extreme attitudes.
4. They act in ways that are consistent with these rigid/extreme attitudes.
5. They rehearse a general version of their specific guilt-based rigid/extreme attitudes so that they easily make guilt-based inferences

about what is generally going on in their life as well as what they are not doing.
6   They develop and rehearse a guilt-based world view.

I will deal with these issues one at a time.

Inferences in guilt

When a person feels guilt, they make one or more inferences about what is going on in the moral domain of their life. Once again these inferences neither have to reflect accurately what the person has done (or not done) or the outcome of their behaviour (or lack of behaviour). The important point is that the person has to believe that they are true. Here is a list of common inferences in guilt:

'I have broken my moral or ethical code'

Here the person breaks their moral code usually by their actions, but it could also be by the thoughts that they have. Here are some examples of this inference:

- Badmouthing a friend to another friend.
- Cheating on one's partner.
- Thinking lewd thoughts about Jesus Christ.

'I have failed to live up to my moral or ethical code'

Here the person fails to act in accord with their moral code. For example:

- Failing to help someone who required assistance.
- Not praying every day.
- Not giving to charity.

'I have harmed or hurt the feelings of others'

Here the person's behaviour or failure to act results in harm or hurt feelings in another person. For example:

- Forgetting one's mother's birthday with the result that she feels hurt.

- Telling one's child off so that they cry.
- Getting someone into trouble at work.

The person holds and rehearses rigid/extreme attitudes towards their inference

Once again, I want to stress that it is not the person's inferences that make the person feel disturbed, since at the heart of their disturbance is a set of rigid/extreme attitudes towards the inferences that they make. In this context, the person will not feel guilty about (a) breaking their moral or ethical code, (b) not living up to their moral or ethical code or (c) harming someone or hurting their feelings without holding rigid/extreme attitudes towards these inferences.

So let me discuss the rigid/extreme attitudes that are at the root of guilt. As with shame, they take the form of a rigid demand and a self-devaluation attitude towards the three inferences that I discussed above. I will outline the general rigid/extreme attitude and illustrate it with a specific example.

Guilt about breaking a moral or ethical code

In general, in order to feel guilty about breaking a moral or ethical code, the person needs to hold a rigid demand about such a code violation (e.g. 'I must not break my moral or ethical code') and a self-devaluation attitude towards this violation (e.g. '...and because I have broken it, I am a bad person'). For example, one of Fiona's moral rules was that it is wrong to let her friends down. On one occasion, she was faced with a choice of getting a free holiday and letting down a friend or supporting her friend and missing out on the holiday. On an impulse she decided to go for the free holiday, which meant that she let down her friend. Fiona made herself guilty about her code violation by holding and practising the following guilt-based rigid/extreme attitude: 'I absolutely should not have let down my friend and because I did, I am a bad person.'

Guilt about not living up to a moral or ethical code

The difference between this situation and the above is that in the above the person has committed a sin (known as the sin of commission), i.e. they have done the wrong thing. Here the person has failed to do the right thing (known as the sin of omission). In general, in order to feel guilty about failing to live up to a moral or ethical code, the person again tends to hold a rigid demand about such a failure (e.g. 'I must live up to my moral or ethical code') and a consequent self-devaluation attitude (e.g. '…and because I have not, I am a bad person'). For example, Roger thinks that going to the aid of someone is the right thing to do. One night Roger saw someone being attacked, but instead of going to the person's aid he turned and walked away from the incident. From his frame of reference, he failed to live up to his ethical code. To feel guilty about his behaviour, Roger brought to the incident the following guilt-based rigid/extreme attitude: 'I absolutely should have gone to the aid of that person and because I didn't, I am a bad person.'

Guilt about harming or hurting the feelings of someone else

In general, in order to feel guilty about harming or hurting the feelings of someone else, a person tends to hold a rigid demand about their role in this situation (e.g. 'I absolutely should not harm or hurt someone') and a self-devaluation attitude towards their role (e.g. '…and because I did, I am a bad person'). For example, Stephanie wanted to visit her parents over Easter, while her partner wanted to visit his in a different part of the country. If Stephanie decided to visit her parents, one way for her to feel guilty about this situation is for her to think, 'My partner is upset and I am the cause', and then to hold the following guilt-based rigid/extreme attitude: 'I upset him, which I must not do, and this proves what a bad, selfish person I am.' Another way for Stephanie to practise this guilt-based rigid/extreme attitude in this situation, but this time without feeling guilty (I call this a way of rehearsing emotional disturbance without feeling it), is for her to go along with her partner's wishes. She would do so because (a) she thinks that he would be upset about not seeing his parents and, more importantly, (b) she would make herself feel guilty about this because she would hold the following guilt-producing rigid/extreme attitude: 'If I went to see my parents, I know that he would be upset and I would be the cause of this. I must not upset my partner and I am a bad, selfish person if I do. Therefore I will go and see his parents.'

The major guilt-based negative self-judgements

As I have shown, when a person feels guilt, the essence of this emotion is the person holding and practising guilt-based rigid/extreme attitudes. Moreover I have stressed that these rigid/extreme attitudes have two major components: a rigid demand and a self-devaluation attitude. A rigid demand, as we have seen, is relatively straightforward. It is absolute and comes in the form of a 'must', 'absolutely should', 'have to', 'got to', amongst others. Self-devaluation attitudes in guilt are a little more varied (although not as varied as in shame) and here I will outline the major guilt-based negative self-judgements.

Before I list these self-devaluation attitudes, remember that a self-devaluation attitude involves a person making a global negative judgement about their entire self. They are not rating a part of themself, they are rating the whole of their 'self'.

'I am bad'

The main form of devaluation of self in guilt is: 'I am bad.' This is sometimes expressed as 'I am a bad person', 'I am rotten' or 'I am a rotten person'. The hallmark of this form of self-devaluation at the point when a person is experiencing guilt is that in their mind their entire 'self' is morally corrupt. Most of the time the person thinks this way after they have (a) broken their moral code, (b) failed to live up to their moral code or (c) harmed or hurt someone's feelings, as I have discussed above. And when the person does so, they make the part–whole error: evaluating their entire self on the basis of one of its parts. In simple terms, the person jumps from 'it's bad' to 'I'm bad'. For example:

- 'Because I stole stationery from my place of work, I am a bad person.'
- 'Because I failed to go to the help of that person being attacked, I am bad.'
- 'Because I hurt my sister's feelings by saying that I didn't like her new dress, I am a rotten person.'

This process of overgeneralising from a part of a person to the whole of them is common to virtually all guilt-based negative self-judgements.

'I am less good than I would have been if...'

Although a person may not condemn themself, they may still make themself feel guilty (although not as guilty as when they do condemn themself) by evaluating themself as less good than they would be if they hadn't done the wrong thing, had done the right thing or hadn't caused harm or hurt to others. For example, if Roger failed to live up to his moral/ethical code by not going to the aid of another person needing help, he can still make himself feel guilty by believing: 'I absolutely should have helped that person and since I didn't, I am less good than I would have been if I had helped him.'

'I am selfish'

One of the characteristics of people who experience chronic guilt (i.e. they feel guilty often and across different situations) is that they tend to be selfless and put the interests of others before their own. When they even think of putting their own healthy interests before the interests of others, they feel guilty and back down because they believe: 'I must make sure that others are catered for before I go for what I want and if I put myself before others, then I am a selfish person.'

The following vignette illustrates this dynamic. Helen was a 40-year-old single woman who was the principal carer for her aging mother with whom she lived. Helen regularly put her mother's interests before her own, with the result that she rarely went out and had virtually no social life. However, she did have two old school friends who were very loyal to her. These friends badgered Helen incessantly to allow them to take her out to celebrate her 40th birthday, even arranging for a professional carer to look after her mother. Eventually, albeit reluctantly, Helen agreed to go after obsessively checking with her mother that she didn't mind. However, just before going into the posh restaurant that her friends had booked for the celebration, Helen made herself feel severely guilty and gave her apologies before rushing home to her mother. Helen did this because she held the following attitude: 'I must not enjoy myself when I know that my mother is not enjoying herself. Because I am putting my pleasure before my mother's feelings, I am a selfish person.'

People like Helen shuttle between two positions in their mind: selflessness and selfishness. When a person does this, they are basically saying that either they put other people's interests before their own or they are a selfish person. What often fuels this attitude is the person's idea that they are unimportant and the only way that they can gain a sense of importance is by ensuring that they help others achieve their goals or that these others don't get upset. Such an idea results in the person becoming highly susceptible to others manipulating them through guilt. Thus, Helen's mother successfully manipulated Helen by saying things like 'Don't worry about me dear, I'll be alright', while giving her a pained expression. What this really meant, as Helen fully realised later, was: 'I'll be upset if you go out and it will be all your fault.'

When an individual believes that they are a selfish person, they are doing three things:

1. They acknowledge that their behaviour is selfish. It often isn't, but the person infers that it is.
2. They assume that because they have acted selfishly, they score highly on the trait known as 'selfishness'.
3. They are using that trait description to define themself. It is as if they are saying:
   'Because I have acted selfishly, I have selfishness and I am therefore a selfish person.' Once the person habitually makes this 'behaviour → trait → self' translation process, they skip the middle step and define their 'self' on the basis of their behaviour [behaviour → self], e.g. 'Because I acted selfishly, I am a selfish person.'

Finally, when an individual believes that they are a selfish person, most of the time they are implying (although they do not make this explicit) that they are a bad person or certainly less good than they would be if they scored highly on selflessness or acted selflessly.

'I don't deserve good things to happen to me. I only deserve bad things...'

Another way that a person can make themself feel unhealthily guilty is to consider themself undeserving of good things, but deserving of bad. This is a more subtle form of self-devaluation and is thus more difficult to identify. But if a person feels guilty and denies the other forms of guilt-based self-devaluation, then this one may well resonate with them.

Unconditional guilt

So far, I have discussed the situation where a person makes themself conditionally guilty, which means that they feel guilty when they hold rigid/extreme attitudes towards:

- Breaking their moral code.
- Failing to live up to their moral code.
- Harming or hurting someone's feelings.

Some people, however, think they are bad people because they are alive, or because of who they are. In other words, their guilt is unconditional. Consequently, like unconditional shame, it is unremitting and ever present.

Thinking that stems from guilt-based rigid/extreme attitudes

When a person holds a guilt-based rigid/extreme attitude towards thinking that (a) they have broken their moral code, (b) they failed to do the right thing and/or (c) they have caused harm or hurt to others, this attitude will influence the way that they subsequently think, as discussed below.

Exaggerating the badness of one's behaviour

Once a person has made themself guilty about their 'sin', they tend to think about what they did in exaggerated ways. In particular, they may think that their actions are much worse than when they first focused on them. Thus, Mary first made herself feel guilty about hurting her parents' feelings by refusing to do their shopping for them. She then exaggerated this by showing herself that her actions were despicably selfish. Having exaggerated the badness of her behaviour in this way, Mary then brought a further guilt-inducing rigid/extreme attitude to this exaggeration, thus making herself even more guilty.

Exaggerating the negative consequences of one's behaviour and minimising its positive consequences

Once a person has made themself feel guilty about their 'sin', they exaggerate the negative consequences of their behaviour and minimise its positive consequences. Thus, Simon made himself feel guilty about stealing stationery from work. Having done so, he thought that he was bound to get caught and would then be fired and find it difficult to get another job (exaggerating the negative consequences of his behaviour). He edited out what he could productively learn from this episode (i.e. that he stole it because he thought he needed it and

Understanding guilt

that he could challenge the attitude that he must have what he wants, minimising the positive consequences of his behaviour).

Assuming more personal responsibility for what happened and assigning less responsibility to others than the situation warrants

Once a person has made themself feel guilty and they look back on their 'sin' and all the factors involved, they tend to assume far more responsibility than the situation warrants and assign far less responsibility to relevant others. They think that it is all their fault.

In addition, the person keeps their feelings of guilt alive by editing out of the picture the responsibility that others have for their own feelings. They do this when they think that they can hurt other people's feelings. Actually, they cannot hurt these other people's feelings. They can treat people badly, harm them physically or materially, but they can't hurt their feelings since these people have the choice whether or not to disturb themselves about the person's behaviour towards them.

Engaging in 'if only' thinking

'If only' thinking serves to perpetuate guilt after the person has begun to experience this emotion. For example, Harold made, in good faith, a business decision that unfortunately did not work out, with the result that he had to sack two of his employees to ensure that his company continued trading. He made himself feel guilty by believing that he absolutely should not have acted in a way that had such bad consequences and that he is a bad person because he did. Harold unwittingly maintained his guilt feelings by showing himself that if only he hadn't acted in that way, he would not have had to sack his two employees. This reinforces Harold's idea that he alone was responsible for sacking his employees. Of course, it may be true that if Harold hadn't made the decision, then the two employees would not have lost their jobs. However, it could equally be true that if Harold hadn't made the decision, then other bad things would have happened such as his company ceasing to trade, putting him and other people out of work.

However, under the influence of his guilt, Harold thought that this bad outcome would not have happened if he hadn't made the decision, and that a good outcome would have happened if he had made a different decision. In doing so, he gave himself a double dose of guilt. First, he made himself feel guilty about the decisions that he took which had a bad outcome: 'I am a bad person because I made a decision that resulted in me having to sack two of my employees. I absolutely should not have made such a bad decision.' Second, he made himself feel guilty for not making a different, more effective decision: 'If only I had made that other investment that I was considering at the time, then I would not have had to lay off my two employees and things would have flourished. I am a bad person for not making the right decision as I absolutely should have done.'

Judging what one did with the benefit of hindsight only

One of the things that people who don't make themselves feel unhealthily guilty do is to look back at their 'sin' from the perspective of when they took action. Thus, they are able to say: 'Yes, I now see that I broke my moral code, but I was so fixated on getting what I wanted, it did not occur to me that I was breaking my moral code. What I have learned from this situation is that I need to deal with my tendency to become fixated so that I can be more aware of the implications of my behaviour.' In contrast, a person who often experiences guilt does not do this. Rather, they only judge their behaviour with the benefit of hindsight (e.g. 'I could have foreseen what I was going to do and therefore I absolutely should have done so' or 'I now see that it would have been better to do "x" rather than "y", therefore I absolutely should have done "y"'). As you can see, hindsight thinking stems from absolute thinking and together they make a very powerful guilt-inducing cocktail. In short, the person believes: 'Because I could have done things differently, I absolutely should have done things differently.'

Not taking into account mitigating factors or showing oneself compassion

Once the person has made themselves feel guilty, they will tend to discount what might be called mitigating factors, i.e. genuine reasons that may help the person take an understanding, compassionate view of their 'sin'. Colloquially, this is called being hard on oneself! If the person believes that they absolutely should not have broken their moral code, such rigidity precludes them from understanding aspects of the situation that may have prompted them to act as they did. This is why I say that guilt and the rigid attitudes upon which it is based are the enemies of understanding.

Failing to appreciate the complexity of the situation

When a person does something wrong, for example, their behaviour is most accurately viewed from a complex perspective. Thus, when Roxanne let down her friend, she faced a choice between letting down her friend and letting down her parents. She decided to let down her friend because she thought that it was the lesser of the two evils. Because she held the attitude 'I must not let down people I care about', she looked at this situation in 'black and white' terms. She concluded: 'Letting down my friend was just plain wrong and that's the end of it. It cannot be justified.'

Thinking that one will receive due retribution for one's behaviour

As I have already discussed, when a person makes themselves feel guilty, one of the guilt-inducing rigid/extreme attitudes that they hold is that they are a bad person. When they think that they are a bad person, this attitude encourages them to think that bad things will happen to them because they think that they deserve retribution for being a bad person. In short, the person believes that bad things happen to bad people because they deserve punishment.

Behaviour that stems from guilt-based rigid/extreme attitudes

When a person holds guilt-based rigid/extreme attitudes, they will tend to act in certain ways. Once again, you will note that many of these behaviours are both an expression of guilt and an attempt by the person to avoid the pain of these feelings. The main point to note is that these behaviours both stem from the person's guilt-based rigid/extreme attitudes and, when they engage in them, help to strengthen their conviction in these attitudes. As such, engaging in guilt-based behaviours renders the person more vulnerable to experiencing guilt.

Confessing regardless of the consequences

Some say that confession is good for the soul and this may be the case if a person thinks carefully about the consequences of their confession and judges that it will do them more good than harm. However, the person who is prone to guilt holds the attitude that they have to confess their 'sin' to the people involved regardless of the consequences. In doing so, they will strengthen their guilt-based rigid/extreme attitude: 'I am a bad person and I must unburden myself to become good again.' Of course, confession (outside a religious context) doesn't lead the person to become good again, and there is a very good chance that the consequences of their confession will be harmful to them and the other(s) involved. This latter point demonstrates how the person can give themself a double dose of guilt: 'I am a bad person for doing what I did in the first place and a bad person for upsetting the other(s) by confessing my sin in the second place.' So, thoughtless confession will lead the person further down the guilt road.

Begging for forgiveness

Another way that a person unwittingly strengthens their guilt-based rigid/extreme attitudes is to beg for forgiveness from the other person that they have wronged, harmed or hurt. In begging rather than asking for forgiveness, the person deepens their conviction that they are a bad despicable creature who can only be raised up if the other person forgives them. If they are not forgiven, they remain a bad person in their mind. If they are forgiven, they feel better temporarily, but since their conviction in their badness remains unchecked, they need frequent reassurance that the other person has still forgiven them. They thus frequently seek reassurance from this other person that they are still forgiven.

Promising unrealistically not to 'sin' again

After the person has wronged, harmed or hurt someone and has made themself feel guilty about doing so, one way that the person attempts to make themself feel better in the short term is to promise the other person that they will not 'sin' again. If the other person accepts their promise, they will feel mightily relieved, but in all probability they won't take steps to put their promise into practice by seeking help to address the factors that led them to 'sin' in the first place. Consequently, they will probably 'sin' again if they encounter these factors and, if they do, they will probably make themself feel guilty for their behaviour all over again. On the other hand, if the other person does not accept their promise, they will not gain this short-term relief and will continue to make themself feel guilty about their 'sin'.

Depriving oneself

When a person has made themself feel guilty, they tend to think that they do not deserve any good things in life. To reinforce this view, they deprive themself of the good things in life. They may not see their friends, for example, and may not engage in any pleasurable activities. In doing so, they implicitly rehearse the view that the reason they are depriving themself is that as a person they do not deserve such pleasure because of their 'sin'.

Punishing oneself

A more extreme version of depriving oneself is punishing oneself. Here the person is not just saying that they do not deserve good things in their life; they are also saying that they deserve bad things in their life. Consequently, the person tends to actively seek out such bad things. For example, they may seek out and spend time with people who actively dislike them or they may engage in tasks that they actively dislike. In doing so, they are acting on the attitude that, because of their 'sin', they deserve to be treated badly by people who dislike them and they are only fit to engage in tasks they hate.

Doing penance

When a person punishes themself for their 'sin', they are, in effect, saying that because they are bad, they deserve to experience bad things. However, when a person does penance for their 'sin' (e.g. deliberately undertaking something onerous), they are saying that they can redeem themself from their badness by their penance. In doing so, they still hold and unwittingly strengthen the attitude that they are a bad person for their 'sin'.

Disclaiming responsibility

When a person has done something wrong, failed to do the right thing or has caused harm or hurt to someone and they hold a guilt-inducing rigid/extreme attitude towards their 'sin', they will *tend to* make themself guilty. I say 'tend to' here because the person can still stop themself from feeling guilty before guilt takes a hold. They can do this by disclaiming responsibility for their actions. Basically, they can do this in two ways. First, they can place the responsibility on some external factor. This might be another person (e.g. 'Yes, I did let you down, but it was my brother's fault; he made me do it') or some aspect of the environment (e.g. 'I would have helped you out, but the train was delayed'). Second, they can place the responsibility on some internal factor such as illness or medication (e.g. 'I don't know what came over me; it must have been the medication I am on'). While the person will not actually experience feelings of guilt if they disclaim responsibility in these ways, they are still rehearsing their guilt-inducing rigid/extreme attitudes, albeit implicitly. For example, when Mark tries to convince himself that the reason why he let down his friend was due to his brother, he is implicitly saying: 'If I acknowledge that I was responsible for letting my friend down, then I would be a bad person. Therefore, to stop blaming myself, I will blame someone else.'

Overcompensating for feelings of guilt

Another way of coping with feelings of guilt is to overcompensate for them. This involves the person doing the very opposite of what they feel guilty about. However, when the person does this, it results in strengthening their guilt-inducing rigid/extreme attitude. Thus, Roberta believed that she is a bad person for having upset her friend. She overcompensated for her guilt feelings by going out of her way to be nice to people. She did that because she thought that the only way that she could get away from the attitude that she is bad was by doing good. However, in doing so, she unwittingly strengthened the idea that her moral worth as a person is based on the way she treats others. This exemplifies the conditional philosophy of guilt: 'I am bad if I treat others badly. I am good if I treat others well.'

Trying to get reassurance from others, but failing to be reassured

After a person has made themself feel guilty for their 'sin', they may be tempted to ask people for reassurance that what they did wasn't wrong, that there was a good reason for what they did, or that they weren't really responsible for their actions. It is likely that they will find plenty of people to give them such reassurance, but they won't stay reassured for long. Holding the attitude that they are a bad person for doing what they absolutely should not have done means that they are not reassurable even if an army of volunteers are recruited to reassure them. It will only take one person to say that what they did was wrong and their guilt-inducing rigid/extreme attitude will lead them back to 'But it was wrong' and from there to: 'Since it was wrong, I absolutely should not have done it, and because I did, I am a bad person.'

The same process happens when another person convinces them for the moment that there was a good reason for what they did or that they weren't really responsible for their actions. Here, as before, the person's guilt-inducing rigid/extreme attitude will lead them to go back and say to themself: 'But there really wasn't a good reason for my behaviour' or 'But I am responsible for my actions'. When they do go back, they will then feel guilty because they will bring their guilt-inducing rigid/extreme attitude to these inferences.

People develop and rehearse general guilt-based rigid/extreme attitudes

General guilt-based rigid/extreme attitudes are rigid/extreme attitudes that a person holds in many theme-related situations that result in them experiencing guilt in these situations. Developing and rehearsing such attitudes will lead the person to experience guilt in many different situations. They will do this mainly because they become practised at inferring, for example, that they have broken their moral or ethical code, failed to live up to their moral or ethical code or caused harm or hurt to relevant others.

Let me show you how this works. First, the person develops general guilt-based rigid/extreme attitudes such as: 'I must never cause hurt or harm to those that I care about and if I do, then this proves that I am a bad person.' They then rehearse these attitudes until they have firm conviction in these attitudes and bring them to relevant situations where it is possible that they caused harm or hurt to relevant others. Then, because they cannot convince themself that they did not harm or hurt the other person, they will tend to think that they have harmed or hurt that person. Having created this guilt-based inference, the person develops and holds a specific version of this general guilt-based rigid/extreme attitude and thereby makes themself feel guilty in this specific situation.

Let me give you a concrete example. Leona developed the following general guilt-based rigid/extreme attitude: 'I must not upset my mother and if I do, I am a bad person.' She took this attitude to a specific situation where her mother asked her over for dinner and she said 'no' because she was going out with a friend that night. She explained this to her mother, but was not sure of her mother's reaction. Her general guilt-based rigid/extreme attitude led her to infer that she upset her mother. It as if she reasoned: 'Because I can't convince myself that I didn't upset my mother, therefore I did.' Her attitude did not allow her to think that her mother was probably OK with her not going to dinner.

Once Leona created her inference, she made herself feel guilty about it by holding a specific version of her general guilt-inducing rigid/extreme attitude: 'I upset my mother by turning down her dinner invitation. I absolutely should not have upset my mother in this way and I am a bad person because I did.' Having made herself feel guilty in this way, Leona then thought and acted in ways that were consistent with her guilt-based rigid/extreme attitude, which had the effect of strengthening this attitude.

People develop and rehearse a view of the world founded on guilt-based rigid/extreme attitudes

I have mentioned several times now that people develop world views that render them vulnerable to particular unhealthy negative emotions. The world views that render a person vulnerable to guilt do so again because they make it very easy for them to make guilt-related inferences. Then, as I have shown you earlier in the chapter, the person makes themself feel guilty about these inferences with the appropriate rigid/extreme attitudes. Here is an illustrative list of guilt-related world views that a person may develop and the inferences that they spawn.

World view: Other people's desires are more important than mine.
Inference: If I put my desires first, I am being selfish.

World view: I have responsibility for the hurt feelings of others.
Inference: If someone's feelings are hurt and I have been involved, then I have hurt that person's feelings.

World view: In the moral domain, I expect more of myself than I do of others.

Inference: There is no excuse for what I did.

In the next chapter, I will help you to understand remorse, which is the healthy alternative to guilt.

Further reading

Academic

Tangney, J.P. & Dearing, R.L. (2002). *Shame and guilt.* New York: Guilford.

Self-help

Dryden, W. (2013). *Coping with guilt.* London: Sheldon.

Chapter 8

Understanding remorse

In this chapter, I will argue that remorse is the healthy emotion alternative to guilt. As with disappointment in Chapter 6, while the components of remorse are clear, the term 'remorse' has not been universally accepted as a plausible name for this emotion. As with shame, some argue that we should use the terms 'unhealthy guilt' and 'healthy guilt' to differentiate between the two emotions and I have no issues with this view (and as I have already mentioned, I use this convention myself later to distinguish between the unhealthy and healthy forms of anger, jealousy and envy). However, in this chapter I will use the term remorse to represent the healthy alternative to guilt.

The components of remorse

When a person feels remorse:

1. They make certain types of inference.
2. They bring remorse-based flexible/non-extreme attitudes to those inferences.
3. They think in ways that are consistent with the above flexible/non-extreme attitudes.
4. They act in ways that are consistent with these flexible/non-extreme attitudes.
5. They use a general version of their specific remorse-based flexible/non-extreme attitudes which helps them to see the world more objectively than when they utilise and rehearse general guilt-based rigid and extreme attitudes.
6. They develop and rehearse a remorse-based world view.

So let me deal with these issues one at a time.

DOI: 10.4324/9781003203483-12

Inferences in remorse

When a person experiences remorse as a healthy alternative to guilt, they make the same inferences as they do when they experience guilt. Again these inferences do not have to reflect accurately what is happening or what has happened. The important point is that the person has to believe that they are true. Here is a reminder of a list of these inferences:[1]

- 'I have broken my moral or ethical code.'
- 'I have failed to live up to my moral or ethical code.'
- 'I have harmed or hurt the feelings of others.'

The person holds and rehearses flexible/non-extreme attitudes towards their inferences

As we have seen, at the core of healthy negative emotions, which are the healthy alternatives to emotional disturbance, the person holds a set of flexible/non-extreme attitudes towards the inferences that they make. In this context, a person will feel remorse about (a) breaking their moral code, (b) failing to live up to their moral code, and/or (c) harming or hurting the feelings of others when they hold flexible/non-extreme attitudes towards these inferences.

So let me discuss which flexible/non-extreme attitudes are at the root of remorse. As you will see, they take the form of a flexible attitude and an unconditional self-acceptance attitude towards the three inferences listed above and discussed in Chapter 7. In the following sections I will outline the general flexible/non-extreme attitude and illustrate it with a specific example.

Remorse about breaking a moral or ethical code

In general, when a person feels remorse about breaking a moral or ethical code, the person holds a flexible attitude towards such a code violation (e.g. 'I really don't want to break my moral or ethical code, but sadly I am not exempt from doing so and nor do I have to be exempt') and an unconditional self-acceptance attitude towards this violation (e.g. '...I am a fallible human being and not a bad person for breaking my code'). For example, Fiona, whom we met in Chapter 7, held to the moral code that it is wrong to let her friends down. If you recall, faced with a choice of getting a free holiday and letting down

120 Guilt and remorse

a friend or supporting her friend and missing out on the holiday, Fiona chose the former. This meant that she let down her friend. For Fiona to feel remorse and not guilt about her code violation, she would need to hold and practise the following remorse-based flexible/non-extreme attitude: 'I really wish that I hadn't let down my friend, that was wrong, but I am not immune from acting badly and neither do I have to be immune. I am not a bad person for letting my friend down. I am a fallible human being who did the wrong thing.'

Remorse about not living up to a moral or ethical code

The difference between this situation and the one above is that in the above the person has committed a sin (known as the sin of commission), i.e. they have done the wrong thing. Here the person has failed to do the right thing (known as the sin of omission). In general, when a person feels remorse about failing to live up to a moral or ethical code, the person again tends to hold a flexible attitude towards such a failure (e.g. 'I want to live up to my moral or ethical code, but I don't have to do so') and a consequent unconditional self-acceptance attitude (e.g. '...I am not a bad person for failing to live up to my moral code. I am a fallible human being who failed to do the right thing.'). For example, as we saw in Chapter 7, Roger values going to the aid of someone and thinks that it is the right thing to do. One night Roger saw someone being attacked, but instead of going to the person's aid he turned and walked away from the incident. From his frame of reference, he failed to live up to his ethical code. In order to feel remorse about his behaviour, Roger would have to bring to the incident the following remorse-based flexible/non-extreme attitude: 'I really wish that I had gone to the aid of that person, but that does not mean that I absolutely should have done so. I am not a bad person for not doing so. I am a fallible human being who failed to do the right thing.'

Remorse about harming or hurting the feelings of someone else

In general, when a person feels remorse about harming or hurting the feelings of someone else, they hold a flexible attitude towards their role in this situation (e.g. 'I much prefer not harming or hurting someone, but sadly that does not mean that I must not do so') and an unconditional self-acceptance attitude towards their role (e.g. '...I am not a bad person for doing so. I am a complex, fallible human being capable of doing such harm and of acting in ways that do not lead to harm.'). For example, remember Stephanie whom we met in the previous chapter. If you recall, she wanted to visit her parents over Easter, while her partner wanted to visit his in a different part of the country. If Stephanie were to feel remorse about this situation, she might still think that she would be the cause if her partner was upset if she decided to visit her parents, but she would hold a flexible/non-extreme attitude towards this: 'I upset him, and I wish I had not done so, but I am not immune from doing so and sadly nor do I have to be so immune. I am not a bad, selfish person, rather I am an ordinary fallible human being who hurt the feelings of a loved one.'

The major attitude towards self in remorse

As we have seen, at the core of remorse a person holds remorse-based flexible/non-extreme attitudes. These flexible/non-extreme attitudes have two major components: a flexible attitude and an unconditional self-acceptance attitude. As I discussed in Chapter 6, a flexible attitude is straightforward in that it is relative and comes in the form of a non-dogmatic preference involving a desire and a negated demand (e.g. 'I want to live up to my moral code, but I don't have to do so'). Unconditional self-acceptance attitudes in remorse are based on the same ideas as those in disappointment (see Chapter 6): that the self is complex and unrateable, fallible and fluid, and that these are the case unconditionally. This contrasts with a self-devaluation attitude in guilt, which involves a person making a global negative judgement about their entire self. The person is not just rating a part of themself, they are rating the whole of themselves.

In remorse, the person does the following:

- Acknowledges the adversity at *A*.
- Negates certain ideas that are present in guilt:
  - 'I am not a bad person.'
  - 'My moral worth as a person does not fluctuate according to my behaviour.'
  - 'I am not a selfish person.'
  - 'I am not undeserving of good things and only deserving of bad things.'
- Asserts who they are: 'I am a complex, unrateable, unique, fluid and fallible human being.'

Thinking that stems from remorse-based flexible/non-extreme attitudes

When a person holds a remorse-based flexible/non-extreme attitude towards thinking that (a) they have broken their moral code, (b) they failed to do the right thing and/or (c) they caused harm or hurt to others, this attitude will influence the way that they subsequently think, as discussed below.

Thinking realistically about the badness of one's behaviour

Once a person has experienced remorse[2] about their 'sin', they tend to think realistically about what they did. In particular, they think that their actions are the same as when they first focused on them and certainly not worse.

Thinking in a balanced way about the negative consequences of one's behaviour and its positive consequences

Once a person has experienced remorse about their 'sin', they are realistic about both the negative and positive consequences of their behaviour. Regarding the latter, the positive consequences concern what a person can productively learn from the experience.

Being balanced when assuming personal responsibility for what happened and when assigning responsibility to others

Once a person has experienced remorse about their 'sin' and considers all the factors involved, they tend to be realistic and balanced when assuming responsibility for their behaviour in the situation and when assigning responsibility to relevant others.

Refraining from engaging in 'if only' thinking

Once the person experiences remorse, they may begin to begin to think in 'if only' terms (see Chapter 7), but they refrain from engaging in such thinking.

Judging what one did from a 'then' perspective with the benefit of hindsight only

One of the things that people who experience remorse rather than guilt think is that they tend to judge what they did from the time perspective of when they took action rather than from a 'now' perspective. Thus remorse encourages a person to say, for example: 'I broke my moral code because I was so fixated on getting what I wanted that it did not occur to me that I was breaking my moral code.' This leads the person to learn from what they did.

Taking into account mitigating factors and showing oneself compassion

When a person feels remorse rather than guilt, they are able to take into account mitigating factors, i.e. genuine reasons that may help the person take an understanding, compassionate view of their 'sin' and why they committed it.

Appreciating the complexity of the situation

When a person does something wrong and they experience remorse, rather than guilt, they can think about their behaviour from a complex perspective as opposed to the 'tunnel vision' thinking that stems from guilt.

Thinking that one may be penalised for one's behaviour rather than receiving retribution

When a person experiences guilt, they tend to think that they are a bad person, which leads them to think that they deserve retribution for being a bad person. When the person experiences remorse, they do not see themselves as bad, but as fallible. This leads them to think that while they may be penalised for their behaviour, they probably won't be punished for it because they don't deserve punishment.

Behaviour that stems from remorse-based flexible/non-extreme attitudes

When a person holds remorse-based flexible/non-extreme attitudes, they will tend to act in certain ways.

Accepting responsibility without self-blame

When a person experiences remorse, they are able to verbally state that they are responsible for their actions without voicing a self-blaming attitude. In guilt, the person would either accept responsibility with self-responsibility or disclaim such responsibility (see Chapter 7).

Confessing while being mindful of the consequences

Remorse-based attitudes may lead the person to confess their 'sin' but with due regard to the consequences of doing so. They will tend to do so when there is a good chance of being forgiven and without being impelled to do so regardless of the consequences, as happens when they hold guilt-based attitudes.

Asking, not begging, for forgiveness and accepting such offers

Remorse-based attitudes will encourage the person to ask for forgiveness from the 'wronged' other, but this is done from a position of healthy responsibility and a wish for reconciliation rather than a desperate need to be forgiven which leads the person to beg for forgiveness.

Also, when the other offers the person their forgiveness, the person graciously accepts it.

Promising to learn from the experience

After the person has wronged, harmed or hurt someone and experiences remorse not guilt, their remorse-based attitudes will lead the person to tell the other that they will resolve to learn from the experience and will not make unrealistic promises that they will not 'sin' again.

Staying connected with good experiences and with others

When a person experiences remorse, they do not think (as they would in guilt) that they do not deserve any good things in life. Consequently, they stay connected with the good that life has to offer and with their friends.

Taking a penalty and making amends

Remorse-based attitudes lead a person to take a penalty and refuse any invitation to punish themself or do penance (i.e. deliberately undertaking something onerous). These attitudes also lead the person to offer to make suitable (i.e. not excessive) amends.

People develop and rehearse general remorse-based flexible/non-extreme attitudes

General remorse-based flexible/non-extreme attitudes are attitudes that a person holds in many theme-related situations that result in them experiencing remorse rather than guilt in these situations. When this is the case, they tend only to infer that they have broken or failed to live up to their moral code or hurt someone when it is clear that such events have occurred. They will then evaluate such situations with specific variants of these general remorse-based flexible/non-extreme attitudes.

People develop and rehearse a view of the world founded on remorse-based flexible/non-extreme attitudes

I have made the point in previous chapters that people develop world views that render them vulnerable to or protect them from particular unhealthy negative emotions. The world views that underpin a person's tendency to experience remorse rather than guilt are as follows, together with the inferences that they spawn.

World view: My desires are important, as are other people's desires. I can assess who I need to prioritise on a case by case basis.
Inference: If I put my desires first, I am probably looking after myself rather than being selfish.

World view: I have responsibility for my actions to others but they ultimately have responsibility for their feelings.
Inference: If someone's feelings are hurt and I have been involved, then I will consider my own actions for their contribution to the other person's hurt feelings, but they need to consider their contribution to their hurt feelings as well.

World view: In the moral domain, being human I expect the same of myself as I do of others.
Inference: There is a reason for what I did.

Notes

1 See Chapter 7 for a discussion of these inferences.
2 When I refer to remorse here, I mean both the emotion and the flexible/non-extreme attitudes that underpin this emotion.

Part 5

Unhealthy anger and healthy anger

Chapter 9

Understanding unhealthy anger

Unhealthy anger is a particularly destructive emotion. It normally has bad psychological and physical effects on the individual and it also sours relationships. Once again I will first outline the general steps that a person tends to take to make themselves feel unhealthily angry before discussing each step in some detail.

Before I do so, let me discuss terminology again. Anger is an easily misunderstood emotion unless we distinguish between unhealthy and healthy anger. By *unhealthy anger* (towards another in this case), I mean a state where the person demands that the other person must or must not act in a certain way and where they condemn the other person for their actions. The person's inclination is to attack the other person in some way and they think that the other has malevolent intent towards them in their actions in the absence of substantiating evidence. By contrast, *healthy anger* is a state where the person prefers the other person to act or not act in a certain way, but does not demand that their preference is met. They evaluate the other person's behaviour as bad, but do not condemn that person for their actions. The person's inclination is to confront the other assertively without attacking them and they do not necessarily think that the other has malevolent intent towards them in their behaviour unless it is clear that this is the case.

The components of unhealthy anger

In order for a person to feel unhealthy anger and stay feeling that way, they tend to do the following:

1 The person makes certain types of inference.

2   They bring a set of unhealthy anger-based rigid/extreme attitudes to those inferences.
3   They think in ways that are consistent with the above rigid/extreme attitudes.
4   They act in ways that are consistent with these rigid/extreme attitudes.
5   They rehearse a general version of their specific unhealthy anger-based rigid/extreme attitudes so that they easily make inferences associated with anger.
6   They develop and rehearse a unhealthy anger-based world view.

Now let me deal with these issues one at a time. As I do so, I will concentrate on how a person makes themself feel unhealthy anger towards others. What I say, however, can easily be generalised so that you can understand how the person makes themself feel unhealthily angry towards themself and towards life conditions.

Unhealthy anger-related inferences

To feel unhealthy anger, the person needs to make one or more inferences about what is going on in their life. Once again these inferences don't have to reflect accurately what happened. The important point is that the person has to believe that they are true. Here is a list of common inferences in unhealthy anger.

Another person (or group of people) transgresses a socially agreed rule, a legal rule or one's own rule

There are socially agreed rules for behaviour, legal rules for behaviour and individuals have their own rules about the people they come into contact with. Here are some examples of others transgressing the above rules:

- Someone jumps a supermarket queue (person breaks socially agreed rule).
- Someone drives through a red light (person breaks legal rule).
- Someone turns up late for an appointment with an individual (person breaks individual's rule).

Being blocked or frustrated in one's progress towards a goal

As humans we all have goals that we strive to achieve. Being blocked or frustrated in our pursuit of our goals often appears in descriptions unhealthy anger episodes. Here are a few examples:

- Being stuck in a traffic jam.
- Another person blocking the person's promotion.
- Missing a train connection.

Injustice/unfairness

A person thinking that they have been treated unjustly or unfairly is a theme that is often found in descriptions of episodes of unhealthy anger. In addition, the person can make themself unhealthily angry about injustice or unfairness that has befallen others. Here are a few examples of each:

- The person being promised a pay rise if they work overtime but not receiving it, even though they kept their side of the bargain.
- Being prosecuted for a crime that the person did not commit.
- Another person being prosecuted for a crime that they did not commit.
- A child being shouted at unfairly by a parent.

Threat to self-esteem

As I will discuss later in this chapter, there is a distinction between unhealthy ego anger and unhealthy non-ego anger. In the former, the person makes themself unhealthily angry about events that impinge on their self-esteem. Here are a number of such events:

- Rejection.
- Being criticised.
- Being ridiculed.

Being treated with disrespect

Being treated with disrespect may be a stimulus for the person making themself unhealthily angry in both ego and non-ego domains.

The person holds and rehearses rigid/extreme attitudes towards their unhealthy anger-related inference

When a person makes themself unhealthily angry, they often state or imply that what happened to them (or their inferences about what happened to them) made them unhealthily angry (e.g. 'Missing the bus made me furious' or 'Your criticism of me made me angry'). As you now know, the person is wrong about this. For it is not what happened to the person or their major inference about that which made them feel unhealthy anger; rather they felt unhealthy anger because of the rigid/extreme attitudes that they held towards the inference that they made. In this context, the person will not feel unhealthily angry about being frustrated, others transgressing their rules, being rejected or criticised, for example, without holding rigid/extreme attitudes towards these inferences.

So let me discuss the rigid/extreme attitudes that are at the core of unhealthy anger.

Two types of unhealthy anger

Before I do so, I want to make an important distinction between two types of unhealthy anger: unhealthy ego anger and unhealthy non-ego anger. When a person makes themself unhealthily angry in the ego domain, they are angry at someone, for example, who has threatened their self-esteem in some way and where at some level they engage in devaluing themself.

By contrast, when the person makes themself unhealthily angry in the non-ego domain, they are angry at someone, for example, who has acted in some way that the person finds offensive, but which does not pose a threat to their self-esteem and where they do not engage in devaluing themself. To complicate matters a little, it is possible for a person to make themself unhealthily angry in both ego and non-ego domains about the same event.

So, as I have stated, it is not what happens to the person or their inference about what happens to them that makes them unhealthily angry; rather, the missing link is their rigid/extreme attitudes towards the actual events or their inferences about these events.

RIGID/EXTREME ATTITUDES IN UNHEALTHY EGO ANGER

So what rigid/extreme attitudes does the person have to hold and rehearse in order to make themselves experience unhealthy ego anger? The following three are the most relevant:

- A rigid demand (e.g. 'You must not criticise me');
- A self-devaluation attitude (e.g. 'Your criticism makes me stupid'); and
- An other-devaluation attitude (e.g. 'You are a bad person for criticising me *and for reminding me that I am stupid*').

RIGID/EXTREME ATTITUDES IN UNHEALTHY NON-EGO ANGER

And how does a person make themself unhealthily angry in the non-ego domain? They do so by holding and rehearsing the following rigid/extreme attitudes:

- A rigid demand (e.g. 'I must get to my meeting on time');
- An unbearability attitude (e.g. 'If I don't get to my meeting on time, I couldn't bear it'); and either
- An other-devaluation attitude (e.g. 'You are rotten for blocking me from getting to my meeting in time', if another person or other people are involved); or
- A life-conditions devaluation attitude (e.g. 'Conditions are rotten for blocking me from getting to my meeting on time').

I will now take the above and show you how a person makes themself unhealthily angry about the inferences that I discussed earlier in the chapter. In doing so, I will outline the general rigid/extreme attitude involved and illustrate it with a specific example.

Unhealthy anger about other(s) transgressing socially agreed rules, legal rules and one's own personal rules

In general, when a person makes themself unhealthily angry about another person, for example, transgressing a socially agreed rule, a legal rule or one of their own rules, they hold a rigid demand about such a transgression and an accompanying other-devaluation attitude.

- 'The person must not jump the queue and they are a selfish rotten person for doing so' (person breaks socially agreed rule).
- 'The person absolutely should not have driven through a red light and is an inconsiderate bastard for doing so' (person breaks legal rule).
- 'The person absolutely should not have turned up late for an appointment with me and is a swine for doing so' (the other breaks the person's own personal rule).

The person will increase their unhealthy anger about these transgressions by holding the following additional rigid/extreme attitude: 'Not only must you not break this rule in the first place, but you must not get away with it without being punished in the second place. If you do get away with it, then that is unfair and this must not be allowed to happen. I can't bear you and the world for allowing you to get away with it.' I will return to this theme of unfairness later in the chapter and show you how a person makes themself unhealthily angry about the injustices and unfairness of life.

Unhealthy anger about being blocked or frustrated in one's progress towards a goal

When a person makes themself unhealthily angry about being blocked or frustrated in their progress towards a goal, they hold a rigid demand and an unbearability attitude. In cases where they consider that another person is responsible for blocking their path towards their goal, the person can make themself unhealthily angry towards the other by additionally holding an other-devaluation attitude. Alternatively, in other cases where the person considers that they themself are responsible for the frustration, then they make themself unhealthily angry at themself by additionally holding a self-devaluation attitude. Here are some examples:

- 'I must not be stuck in the traffic jam (rigid demand) and I can't stand it that I am (unbearability attitude). Whoever is responsible for this is a bastard (other-devaluation attitude).'
- 'Fred blocked my promotions. He absolutely should not have done this (rigid demand) and he is a swine for doing so (other-devaluation attitude).'
- 'I missed my train connection because I left home too late. I absolutely should not have done this (rigid demand) and I am an idiot for doing so (self-devaluation attitude).'

Unhealthy anger about injustice or unfairness

In general, in order to make themself unhealthily angry about injustice or unfairness, a person once again needs to hold a rigid demand and an unbearability attitude towards such a situation and a devaluation attitude towards the person, people or organisation they deem to be responsible for the injustice/unfairness. For example:

- 'I was promised a raise if I worked overtime. I worked overtime but was not given the promised raise. My boss absolutely should not be so unfair to me (rigid demand). It is unbearable (unbearability attitude) and he is a bastard for breaking his promise (other-devaluation attitude).'
- 'I was prosecuted for a crime that I did not commit. The justice system stinks for doing something to me (devaluation attitude towards life conditions) that it absolutely should not have done (rigid demand).'
- 'A colleague of mine was prosecuted for a crime that she did not commit. The police are bastards (other-devaluation attitude) for doing something to her that they absolutely should not have been allowed to get away with (rigid demand). I can't bear this injustice (unbearability attitude).'

Unhealthy anger about a threat to self-esteem

When a person makes themself unhealthily angry about a threat to their self-esteem, they tend to hold three rigid/extreme attitudes: (a) a rigid demand about the other threatening their self-esteem, (b) an other-devaluation attitude towards this other person and (c) a self-devaluation attitude (usually well hidden) that renders the person vulnerable to the threat in the first place. Let me give you an example.

Someone criticised Brenda, who felt unhealthily angry about this criticism. She made herself unhealthily angry about this because:

- She devalued herself about this criticism by holding the following rigid/extreme attitude: 'I must not be criticised and if I am, it proves that I am an inadequate person.'
- She quickly covered up her feelings of inadequacy by holding the person who criticised her responsible for her feelings and devalued that person as in the following rigid/extreme attitude: 'You must not criticise me and remind me that I am an inadequate person and you are no good for doing so.'

Unhealthy anger about being treated with disrespect

When the person makes themselves unhealthily angry about being treated with disrespect, that issue could be ego-based or non-ego-based. When it is ego-based, the person holds:

- The rigid/extreme attitude that the other must treat them with respect and if the other doesn't, this proves that they themself are not worthy of respect; or
- The rigid/extreme attitude that the other must not treat them with disrespect and by doing so the other is a bastard for reminding them that they are not worthy of respect when they are disrespected.

If the issue is non-ego-based, the person's major concern is that the other has transgressed their rule for being treated with respect. Thus, in order to make themselves unhealthily angry about this, the person holds a rigid demand that the other person must not treat them with disrespect and that the other is a bastard for so doing. In non-ego unhealthy anger about disrespect the person does not hold a self-devaluation attitude.

Thinking that stems from unhealthy anger-based rigid/extreme attitudes

When a person holds an unhealthy anger-based rigid/extreme attitude towards any of the factors I discussed earlier in the chapter, this attitude will influence how they subsequently think in the following ways.

Overestimating the extent to which the other person acted deliberately and with malice towards one

After the person has made themselves unhealthily angry about the wrong that another person has done to them, for example, and they reflect on what that person has done, they are likely to conclude (a) that the other acted deliberately in that way towards them (rather than accidentally or because the other saw things differently from the person) and (b) that the other's behaviour was motivated with malicious intent. It may well be that the person thought that way originally and that this was a central feature of what they were unhealthily angry about; however, their rigid/extreme attitude would strengthen their conviction that the other person was deliberately out to get them. Also the person's rigid/extreme attitude would lead them to dwell on this inference for quite a while and increase the likelihood that they would believe that they must exact revenge on the other person, thus deepening their unhealthy anger.

Viewing oneself as definitely right and the other person as definitely wrong

Once the person has made themself unhealthily angry about different versions that they and someone else had about an event, their unhealthy anger-based rigid/extreme attitude will strengthen them in the idea that they were in the right and that the other person was in the wrong. They will then tend to focus on this and hold the following rigid/extreme attitudes:

- 'The other person absolutely should not have been wrong in the first place.'

and as the other attempts to persuade the person that they were right and the person was wrong:

- 'The other person must listen to reason and admit that they were wrong.'

Refusing to listen to or see the other person's point of view

When a person holds a unhealthy anger-based rigid/extreme attitude towards what someone else has done and is in dialogue with that person, they focus on communicating why they are right and as such they will tend to refuse to listen to the other person's point of view. Even if they do listen to the other person, their unhealthy anger will interfere with their attempt to understand this viewpoint. The other is wrong and thus their explanations are not worthy of consideration.

Developing and rehearsing revenge fantasies

Imagination is a powerful tool. Once a person is unhealthily angry, they will tend to use their imagination to develop and rehearse fantasies of exacting revenge. What the person does is this:

1. They focus on the situation where another person has wronged them.
2. They bring their unhealthy anger-creating rigid/extreme attitude to this inference, for example: 'The other person absolutely should not have wronged me and they are a bastard for so doing.'
3. They show themself that justice has to be achieved and that they have to get their revenge.
4. They think of ways of getting revenge and develop scenarios where they see themself, in their mind's eye, exacting revenge on the person who has wronged them.
5. They focus on the sense of pleasure and power they get when seeing themself, in their mind's eye, exacting revenge.

Every time the person rehearses a revenge fantasy, they strengthen their conviction in the following two unhealthy anger-creating rigid/extreme attitudes:

- 'The other person is bad for doing what they absolutely should not have done to me.'
- 'When someone wrongs me, I must get my own back and punish that person.'

Behaviour that stems from unhealthy anger-based rigid/extreme attitudes

When a person holds unhealthy anger-based rigid/extreme attitudes, they will tend to act in certain ways. When they do act in these ways, they rehearse and therefore strengthen their conviction in these rigid/extreme attitudes.

Blaming the other person for making one unhealthily angry

When the person discusses their unhealthily angry feelings with friends and acquaintances, they tend to place the blame for their angry feelings on the behaviour of the person with whom they are unhealthily angry. They say things like: 'They made me angry.' As it is unlikely that their friends will contradict them, this faulty notion remains unchecked and they will continue to refrain from taking responsibility for making themself unhealthily angry.

Understanding unhealthy anger 139

In dialogue with the other person at whom they are unhealthily angry, the person will also blame the other person for making them angry.

Attacking the other person verbally

After the person has made themself unhealthily angry about what another person has done to them, for example, they will feel an urge to attack that person verbally. This can involve shouting and screaming at the person, making pejorative comments or just being generally unpleasant. When the person does some or all of these things, one of two things will happen. First, the other person may well make themself unhealthily angry about the verbal attack and attack the person back. If this happens, then it is likely that the first person will make themself unhealthily angry about the verbal counter-attack and will shout and scream back even more. Second, the other person may display signs that they feel hurt about the person's angry attacking behaviour. This then serves as a stimulus for the person to make themself feel guilty for hurting the other person's feelings (see Chapter 7).

Pursuing revenge

Revenge is sweet and pursuing it will certainly serve to strengthen the person's unhealthy anger-related rigid/extreme attitudes. When the person pursues revenge directly (by which I mean that the other person knows that they were the person who meted out revenge), they not only hold the attitude that the other person absolutely should not have wronged them in the way that they did, but they also hold one or more of the following rigid/extreme attitudes:

- 'The other person absolutely must not get away with their bad behaviour towards me.'
- 'The wrong towards me must be put right.'
- 'They must be punished for their behaviour towards me.'
- 'I must be the one to punish the other person and they must know that it was me who did it.'

Attacking the other person passive-aggressively

Gaining revenge can also be achieved indirectly. This is known as passive-aggressive behaviour and it also serves to reinforce the person's unhealthy anger-creating rigid/extreme attitudes. When a person is passive-aggressive in their attacks, they get revenge against the other person who realises that someone has attacked them but doesn't know who. As such, the person is acting on the following rigid/extreme attitudes:

- 'The other person absolutely must not get away with their bad behaviour towards me.'
- 'The wrong towards me must be put right.'
- 'The other person must be punished for their behaviour towards me, but they must not know that I am the person who has attacked them.'

Recruiting allies against the other person

Another good way of paying someone back and strengthening the person's conviction in their unhealthy anger-creating rigid/extreme attitudes is to recruit allies against the other person. This may involve the person recruiting people to engage in a direct vengeful attack on the other, to deprive that person of their place in a social group or to besmirch the reputation of that person in the social community. In all three cases the person will be acting on the rigid/extreme attitude that the other person absolutely should not have wronged them or their reference group, is a bad person for so doing and thereby deserves to be paid back for their behaviour.

Expressing one's unhealthy anger cathartically

The counselling and psychotherapy field used to think that it was healthy for the person to express their unhealthy anger and that if they didn't, then they would turn their anger towards themself and make themself feel depressed. However, we now know that expressing unhealthy anger cathartically (i.e. with fully expressed feeling) only serves to make a person even angrier (in the unhealthy sense). This is because as the person expresses their unhealthy anger, they are rehearsing and thereby reinforcing their unhealthy anger-creating rigid/extreme attitudes. The answer to the question 'How do you get to Carnegie Hall?' is 'Practise, practise, practise'. Similarly, the answer to the question 'How do you make yourself unhealthily angry?' is 'Practise, practise, practise'. One way of practising is to express unhealthy anger cathartically.

Displacing one's unhealthy anger or 'kick the cat'

You have probably heard the phrase 'kicking the cat'. This refers to times when a person takes their unhealthy anger out on an innocent bystander. Doing so serves to reinforce their unhealthy anger-related rigid/extreme attitudes in a similar way to cathartic expression of unhealthy anger. When a person 'kicks the cat', they are expressing their unhealthy anger indirectly at the person with whom they have a problem. They do not express their unhealthily angry feelings directly at the other person for a number of reasons, with anxiety heading the list.

Withdrawing aggressively

A final way in which the person acts when they are unhealthily angry, thus strengthening their unhealthy anger-creating rigid/extreme attitudes and thus making themself more prone to unhealthy anger, is to withdraw aggressively from situations in which they have made themself unhealthily angry. The person tends to do this by leaving situations in which they feel unhealthy anger, demonstrating non-verbally that they are unhealthily angry. Brian, for example, used to make himself unhealthily angry in business meetings and stormed out of these meetings by banging the door as hard as he could. Eventually he received verbal and written warnings about this, before he sought help for his problem anger.

People develop and rehearse general unhealthy anger-based rigid/extreme attitudes

General unhealthy anger-based rigid/extreme attitudes are rigid/extreme attitudes that a person holds in many theme-related situations that result in them experiencing unhealthy anger in these situations. Developing and rehearsing such attitudes will lead the person to experience unhealthy anger in many different situations. They will do this mainly because they tend to make inferences, for example, that others have transgressed socially agreed, legal or their own personal rules, that others have frustrated their goal-directed efforts, that others have behaved unjustly or unfairly to the person and/or to others, and that others are posing a threat to the person's self-esteem.

Let me show you how this works. First, the person develops general unhealthy anger-based rigid/extreme attitudes such as: 'Other people must obey the rules and they are rotten people if they don't.' They then rehearse this general attitude until they have strong conviction in it and bring it to relevant situations where it is possible that others may not obey the rules. Then, because the person cannot convince themself that the other will obey the rules, they tend to think that the other has disobeyed the rules and done so intentionally and with malicious intent. Having created this unhealthy anger-based inference, the person then brings a specific version of this general unhealthy anger-based rigid/extreme attitude to it and thereby makes themself feel unhealthy anger in the specific situation.

Let me give you a concrete example. Terence developed the following general unhealthy anger-based rigid/extreme attitude: 'Others must respect me and if they don't, I am not worthy of respect and they are no good for demonstrating this.' He took this attitude to a specific situation where he was in a restaurant with a group of friends and a waiter asked everybody else for their order, but didn't ask Terence for his. His general unhealthy anger-based rigid/extreme attitude led him to infer that the waiter showed him disrespect by not asking him for his order. It as if Terence reasoned: 'Because I can't convince myself that the waiter's failure to ask me for my order was an innocent error, then it proves that he showed me disrespect.' Terence's attitude did not allow him to think that the waiter may have made a mistake.

Once Terence created his inference that he had been disrespected, he made himself unhealthily angry about it by holding a specific version of his general rigid/extreme attitude: 'The waiter showed me disrespect by not asking me for my order. He absolutely should have shown me respect and because he didn't, I am not a person worthy of respect and he is no good for demonstrating this.'

People develop and rehearse a view of the world founded on unhealthy anger-based rigid/extreme attitudes

As discussed several times before, people develop world views that render them vulnerable to particular unhealthy negative emotions. This is certainly the case with unhealthy anger. The world views that render a person vulnerable to unhealthy anger do so primarily because they make it very easy for them to make unhealthy anger-related inferences. Then, as I have shown you earlier in the chapter, the person makes themself unhealthily angry about these inferences with the appropriate rigid/extreme attitudes. Here is an illustrative list of the unhealthy anger-related world views that a person develops and the inferences that they spawn.

World view: It's a dog eat dog world.
Inference: People's actions will often be vicious and attacking.

World view: People only look after themselves and their own.
Inference: People's motives are primarily influenced by selfishness.

World view: There's no such thing as an accident. People always act with deliberation.
Inference: When people transgress the rules, they do so deliberately.

World view: People are out to get me, so I need to get them before they get me.
Inference: People's actions are designed to harm me.

In the next chapter, I will help you to understand healthy anger, the healthy alternative to unhealthy anger.

Further reading

Academic

DiGiuseppe, R. & Tafrate, R.C. (2007). *Understanding anger disorders.* New York: Oxford University Press.

Self-help

Dryden, W. (1997). *Overcoming anger: When anger helps and when it hurts.* London: Sheldon.

Chapter 10

Understanding healthy anger

In this chapter, I will argue that healthy anger (sometimes referred to as 'non-problematic anger') is the healthy emotion alternative to unhealthy anger. As with a number of healthy emotion alternatives to unhealthy emotions, while the components of healthy anger are clear (see below), the best term for describing a healthy form of anger is disputed. There is certainly no universal agreement on what such a term would be. In Chapter 9, I referred to the unhealthy form of anger as 'unhealthy anger', so in this chapter I will refer to its healthy alternative as 'healthy anger'.

The components of healthy anger

In order for a person to feel healthy anger and maintain this emotion, they tend to do the following:

1 They make certain types of inference.
2 They bring a set of healthy anger-based flexible/non-extreme attitudes to those inferences.
3 They think in ways that are consistent with the above flexible/non-extreme attitudes.
4 They act in ways that are consistent with these flexible/non-extreme attitudes.
5 They rehearse a general version of their specific healthy anger-based flexible/non-extreme attitudes which helps them to see the world more objectively than when they utilise and rehearse general unhealthy anger-based rigid and extreme attitudes.
6 They develop and rehearse a healthy anger-based world view.

Now let me deal with these issues one at a time. As I do so, I will concentrate on how a person makes themself feel healthy anger towards others. What I say, however, can easily be generalised so that you can understand how the person makes themself feel healthily angry towards themself and towards life conditions.

Inferences in healthy anger

When a person experiences healthy anger as a healthy alternative to unhealthy anger, they make the same inferences as they do when they experience unhealthy anger. Again these inferences do not have to reflect accurately what is happening or what has happened. The important point is that the person has to believe that they are true. Here is a reminder of a list of these inferences:[1]

- Another person (or group of people) transgresses a socially agreed rule, a legal rule or one's own rule.
- Being blocked or frustrated in one's progress towards a goal.
- Injustice/unfairness.
- Threat to self-esteem.
- Being treated with disrespect.

The person holds and rehearses flexible/non-extreme attitudes towards the inference

As we have seen, at the core of healthy negative emotions, which are the healthy alternatives to emotional disturbance, the person holds a set of flexible/non-extreme attitudes towards the inferences that they make. In this context, a person will feel unhealthy anger when they make one or more of the above inferences *and* when they hold flexible/non-extreme attitudes towards these inferences.

So let me discuss which flexible/non-extreme attitudes are at the root of healthy anger.

Two types of healthy anger

Before I do so, I want to make an important distinction between two types of healthy anger: healthy ego anger and healthy non-ego anger. When a person makes themself healthily angry in the ego domain, they are healthily angry when someone, for example, has threatened their self-esteem in some way but where they accept themself unconditionally in the face of this threat.

By contrast, when the person makes themself healthily angry in the non-ego domain, they are healthily angry when someone, for example, has acted in some way that the person finds offensive, but which does not pose a threat to their self-esteem. To complicate matters a little, it is possible for a person to make themself healthily angry in both ego and non-ego domains about the same event.

So, as I have stated, it is not what happens to the person or their inference about what happens to them that makes them healthily angry. Rather, the missing link is their flexible/non-extreme attitudes towards the actual events or their inferences about these events.

FLEXIBLE/NON-EXTREME ATTITUDES IN HEALTHY EGO ANGER

So what flexible/non-extreme attitudes does the person have to hold and rehearse in order to make themselves experience healthy ego anger? The following three are the most relevant:

- A flexible attitude (e.g. 'I don't want you to criticise me, but that does not mean that you must not do so');
- An unconditional self-acceptance attitude (e.g. 'I don't like your criticism, but it does not make me stupid. I am the same unrateable fallible human being whether or not you criticise me'); and
- An unconditional other-acceptance (e.g. 'You are not a bad person for criticising me. You are fallible and even if you think I am stupid, I am not').

FLEXIBLE/NON-EXTREME ATTITUDES IN HEALTHY NON-EGO ANGER

And how does a person make themself healthily angry in the non-ego domain? They do so by holding and rehearsing the following flexible/non-extreme attitudes:

- A flexible attitude (e.g. 'I want to get to my meeting on time, but I don't have to so');
- A bearability attitude (e.g. 'If I don't get to my meeting on time, it's a struggle for me to bear it, but I could do so'). Also it is worth it for me to bear being late, and I am both willing to do so and am going to do so; and either
- An unconditional other-acceptance attitude (e.g. 'You are fallible and not rotten for blocking me from getting to my meeting in time', if another person or other people are involved); or

- An unconditional life-conditions acceptance attitude (e.g. 'Conditions are a mixture of the good, the bad and the neutral even when they block me from getting to my meeting on time').

I will now take the above and show you how a person can make themself healthily angry about the inferences that I discussed earlier in the chapter. In doing so, I will outline the general flexible/non-extreme attitude involved and illustrate it with a specific example.

Healthy anger about other(s) transgressing socially agreed rules, legal rules and one's own personal rules

In general, when a person makes themself healthily angry about another person, for example, transgressing a socially agreed rule, a legal rule or one of their own rules, they hold a flexible attitude towards such a transgression and an accompanying unconditional other-acceptance attitude.

- 'I would much prefer it if the other person did not jump the queue, but they don't have to abide by this convention. They may be acting selfishly by doing so, but they are not a selfish rotten person for doing so. Rather, they are a fallible, complex person who is doing the wrong thing' (person breaks socially agreed rule).
- 'It would have been highly desirable if the person had not driven through a red light, but they don't have to do what is highly desirable. They are not an inconsiderate bastard for doing so. They are an ordinary person who has acted inconsiderately' (person breaks legal rule).
- 'I really don't like it when the person turned up late for an appointment with me, but they do not have to share my views on time-keeping. The other is not a swine for doing so. Rather they are fallible and in my view have acted poorly' (the other breaks the person's own personal rule).

Healthy anger about being blocked or frustrated in one's progress towards a goal

When a person makes themself healthily angry about being blocked or frustrated in their progress towards a goal, they hold a flexible attitude and a non-extreme bearability attitude. In cases where they consider that another person is responsible for blocking their path towards their goal, the person can make themself healthily angry towards the other by additionally holding an unconditional other-acceptance attitude. Alternatively, in other cases where the person considers that they themself are responsible for the frustration, then they make themself healthily angry at themself by additionally holding an unconditional self-acceptance attitude. Here are some examples:

- 'I would prefer not to be stuck in a traffic jam, but it does not follow that I am must not be thus stuck (flexible attitude). It's difficult for me to put up with this, but I can do so. Furthermore, it's worth it to me to do so, I am willing to do so and I am going to do so (bearability attitude). Whoever is responsible for this is not a bastard. They are human who may have done something stupid or may not have done. I just don't know (unconditional other-acceptance attitude).'
- 'Fred blocked my promotions. I really wish he had not done this, but sadly there is no law which states that he must not have done so (flexible attitude). Fred is not a swine for doing so. He is a fallible human being who acted against me on these occasions, but has helped me in the past (unconditional other-acceptance attitude).'
- 'I missed my train connection because I left home too late. I would have preferred not to have done this, but that does not mean that I absolutely should not have done so (flexible attitude). I may have acted idiotically on this occasion, but I am not an idiot for doing so. I am a fallible, complex human being capable of acting idiotically and intelligently (unconditional self-acceptance attitude).'

Healthy anger about injustice or unfairness

In general, in order to make themself healthily angry about injustice or unfairness, a person once again needs to hold a flexible attitude and a non-extreme bearability attitude towards such a situation and an unconditional acceptance attitude towards the person, people or organisation they deem to be responsible for the injustice/unfairness. For example:

- 'I was promised a raise if I worked overtime. I worked overtime but was not given the promised raise. I wish my boss had not been so unfair to me, but unfortunately he does not have to keep his promise (flexible attitude). It is a struggle for me to bear his behaviour, but I can do so, it is in my interests to do so, I am willing to do so and furthermore I am going to do so (bearability attitude). My boss is not a bastard for breaking his promise. He is a fallible human being capable of acting fairly and unfairly (unconditional other-acceptance attitude).'

- 'I was prosecuted for a crime that I did not commit. The justice system can be good and it can be bad and in this case it was bad for what it did to me (unconditional acceptance attitude towards life conditions). I wish it did not do this, but sadly it does not have to be the way I want it to be (flexible attitude).'
- 'A colleague of mine was prosecuted for a crime that she did not commit. The police are not bastards for treating her so badly even though I think that their behaviour was bastardly (unconditional other-acceptance attitude). I really don't want them to get away with this, but sadly that does not mean that this must not happen (flexible attitude). I can bear this injustice even though it is difficult. It's worth it to me to bear it as doing so will help keep me focused on the fight for justice. So I am willing to bear their behaviour and I am going to do so (bearability attitude).'

Healthy anger about a threat to self-esteem

When a person makes themself healthily angry about a threat to their self-esteem, they tend to hold three flexible/non-extreme attitudes: (a) a flexible attitude towards the other threatening their self-esteem, (b) an unconditional other-acceptance attitude towards this other person and (c) an unconditional self-acceptance attitude. Let me give you an example.

Someone criticised Brenda, who felt healthily angry about this criticism. She made herself healthily angry about this because:

- She accepted herself unconditionally about this criticism by holding the following flexible/non-extreme attitude: 'I don't want to be criticised, but that does not mean that it must not happen. The other's criticism does not prove that I am an inadequate person. I am acceptable as a human whether or not I am criticised.'

Healthy anger about being treated with disrespect

When the person makes themself healthily angry about being treated with disrespect, that issue can be ego-based or non-ego-based. When it is ego-based, the person holds:

- The flexible/non-extreme attitude that it is preferable for the other to treat them with respect, but they don't have to do so. If they don't, this does not prove that they themself are not worthy of respect. Rather they are worthy of respect because they are human and alive irrespective of whether they are respected or disrespected; or
- The flexible/non-extreme attitude that it is preferable for the other not to treat them with disrespect, but there is no law that states that they must not do so. If they do so, the other is not a bastard for inviting them to consider themself not worthy of respect. First, they are a fallible human and not a bastard and, second, the person can decline the other's invitation and choose to view themself as worthy of respect no matter what.

If the issue is non-ego-based, the person's major concern is that the other has transgressed their rule for being treated with respect. However, in order to make themself healthily angry about this, the person holds a flexible attitude that it is preferable that the other person not treat them with disrespect, but they don't have to do what is preferable, and that they are flawed and fallible and not a bastard for so doing.

Thinking that stems from healthy anger-based flexible/non-extreme attitudes

When a person holds a healthy anger-based rigid/extreme attitude towards any of the factors I discussed earlier in the chapter, this attitude will influence how they subsequently think in the following ways.

Being realistic and balanced about the intent of the other person and the extent to which the other person acted deliberately and with malice towards one

After the person has made themself healthily angry about the wrong that another person has done to them, for example, and they reflect on what that person has done, they are likely to conclude (a) that the other may have acted deliberately in that way towards them, but that it is just as possible that their actions were accidental or stemmed from a different way of viewing the situation, and (b) that the other's behaviour may have been motivated with malicious intent, but it is just as possible that such intent was not present.

Viewing oneself as probably but not definitely right and the other person as probably but not definitely wrong

Once the person has made themselves healthily angry about different versions that they and someone else had about an event, their healthy anger-based flexible/non-extreme attitude will open them to the possibility that they may be in the wrong and that the other person may be in the right, even though they are reasonably certain that this is not the case.

Open to listening to or seeing the other person's point of view

When a person holds a healthy anger-based flexible/non-extreme attitude towards what someone else has done and is in dialogue with that person, they become open to listening to the other person and understanding their point of view.

Adopting a problem-solving mindset

When the person is operating according to unhealthy anger-related attitudes, as we saw in Chapter 9, they are preoccupied with matters such as getting even and gaining revenge. These states are not conducive to effective problem-solving thinking. However, the flexibility and non-extreme nature of the attitudes related to healthy anger do help the person to concentrate on the situation about which they are healthily angry and then to access the part of their mind that can think about solving the problem.

Behaviour that stems from healthy anger-based flexible/non-extreme attitudes

When a person holds healthy anger-based flexible/non-extreme attitudes, they will tend to act in certain ways. When they do act in these ways, they rehearse and therefore strengthen their conviction in flexible/non-extreme attitudes.

Asserting oneself in a non-blaming way towards the other

When the person discusses their healthy angry feelings, they will communicate in an assertive, non-blaming way towards the other person. Healthy assertion comprises: (a) clear communication where the speaker takes responsibility for their healthy anger; (b) a descriptive account of the behaviour of the other about which the person is healthily angry; (c) a non-demanding request that the other person change. If the person experiences unhealthy anger, they would not be able to sustain assertive communication with the other even if they resolve to do so.

Implementing a problem-solving mindset

As I mentioned above, when a person holds a set of flexible and non-extreme attitudes related to healthy anger, they can adopt a problem-solving thinking mindset. Holding these attitudes in place will help the person to implement this mindset and try out possible solutions to the situation about which they are healthily angry.

Withdrawing non-aggressively

If the person has tried to assert themself with the other person and/or has tried to implement a solution to the problematic situation and these endeavours have failed, then the person will be able to withdraw from the situation non-aggressively if they hold flexible/non-extreme attitudes related to healthy anger. Contrast this with them withdrawing aggressively when they hold rigid/extreme attitudes associated with unhealthy anger.

People develop and rehearse general healthy anger-based flexible/non-extreme attitudes

General healthy anger-based flexible/non-extreme attitudes are attitudes that a person holds in many theme-related situations that result in them experiencing healthy anger rather than unhealthy anger in these situations. When they do this, they only make anger-related inferences when it is clear that such events have occurred. They will then evaluate such situations with specific variants of these general healthy anger-based flexible/non-extreme attitudes.

People develop and rehearse a view of the world founded on healthy anger-based flexible/non-extreme attitudes

I have made the point in previous chapters that people develop world views that render them vulnerable to or protect them from particular unhealthy negative emotions. The world views that underpin a person's tendency to experience healthy anger rather than unhealthy anger are as follows, together with the inferences that they spawn.

World view: It's a world where people can be supportive towards one another or attack one another.
Inference: People's actions can be vicious and attacking, but they can also be kind and supportive.

World view: People look after themselves and their own and they look after others as well.
Inference: People's motives can be influenced by selfishness, but they can also be influenced by kindness and caring.

World view: Accidents do sometimes happen. People can act with deliberation, but they can also act so that accidents occur.
Inference: When people transgress the rules, they may have done so deliberately, but there are many other reasons that explain their actions.

World view: People may be out to get me, but most people don't have this motivation.
Inference: Sometimes people's actions are designed to harm me, but most of the time they aren't.

Note

1 See Chapter 9 for a discussion of these inferences.

Part 6

Hurt and sorrow

Chapter 11

Understanding hurt

Hurt is an unhealthy negative emotion that a person is most likely to feel about the way that people significant to them behave (or fail to behave). I will follow the usual format in this chapter by first outlining the components of hurt, before discussing each component in some detail.

The components of hurt

In order for a person to feel hurt and stay feeling that way, they tend to do the following:

1   The person makes certain types of inference.
2   They bring a set of hurt-based rigid/extreme attitudes to those inferences.
3   They think in ways that are consistent with the above rigid/extreme attitudes.
4   They act in ways that are consistent with these rigid/extreme attitudes.
5   They rehearse a general version of their specific hurt-based rigid/extreme attitudes so that they easily make hurt-related inferences.
6   They develop and rehearse a hurt-based world view.

Now let me deal with these issues one at a time.

Inferences in hurt

In order to feel hurt, a person needs to make one or more inferences about what is going on in their life. As I have repeatedly stressed,

DOI: 10.4324/9781003203483-17

these inferences don't have to reflect accurately what happened. The important point is that the person believes that they are true.

What people tend to feel hurt about is what others (usually significant others) have done or have failed to do. What follows is a list of common hurt-related inferences about what people have done. It is important to note that the person feeling hurt considers that they do not deserve such behaviour at the hands of the other person. Indeed, it is very likely that the person considers that they deserve the very opposite. In certain respects, the following inferences can be subsumed under the general heading 'I am more invested in our relationship than the other person is'.

Being unfairly criticised

While a person can feel hurt about unfair or fair criticism, they are more likely to feel hurt about a significant other criticising them unfairly. In addition, the person is more likely to feel hurt about criticism that is directed to them as a person rather than criticism that is directed at their behaviour.

Being rejected

What a person finds particularly hurtful about being rejected is often the undeserved nature of the rejection. In doing so, the person tends to remind themself of all the good things that they have done for the other person and how they deserve far better. The person tends to edit out all the things they may have done (or not done) that may have brought about their rejection.

Sharon tended to ask her partner for things at very inconvenient times for him. She edited out the fact that her request was unreasonable and focused instead (a) on the fact that she was rejected and (b) on how she did not deserve to be rejected. Rather, she thought that she deserved to have her request met after all she had done for her partner in the past. For example, Sharon made sexual overtures to her partner at a time when he was exhausted and unlikely to respond sexually to her. In feeling hurt about being rejected, Sharon forgot about the untimeliness of her request and instead told herself that she had gone to a lot of trouble to make life pleasant for her partner and the least she deserved was some pleasure in return.

Being disapproved by the other person

Disapproval is similar to rejection in that both involve another making some kind of negative judgement of the person, but they are different in that in rejection the other has cast the person aside, which the other hasn't done yet when they disapprove of the person. As with rejection, the person tends to feel more hurt when they think that the disapproval they have received is undeserved. Also, as with hurt, the person focuses on the undeserved nature of the disapproval rather than on what they may have done to provoke it.

Being betrayed by the other

Being betrayed by someone close to the person is a key hurt-related inference. Gina was a person who considered that she had been betrayed a lot in her life. On examination, this is what she tended to do. She placed absolute trust in people close to her and then told them all about her past, swearing them all not to tell a living soul. One or two people would violate this promise (but most wouldn't). Gina focused on the one or two that had 'betrayed' her and made herself feel hurt about this betrayal. What Gina did not appreciate was that if one takes a large number of people into one's confidence, statistically it is likely that one or two would break confidentiality. However, Gina focused on the betrayal rather than on the dubious wisdom of indiscriminate secret-sharing.

The remainder of this list of hurt-related inferences concerns what other people fail to do. Once again, it is important to note that the person feeling hurt is likely to consider that they deserve far better treatment than they are getting from the other person.

Being neglected

A person inferring that they have been neglected by someone close to them is a common hurt-related inference. People who consider that they have been neglected by others often play a part in this neglect. For example, Barbara used to take the lead with all of her friends in making social arrangements and continued to do this for a long period until her friends had grown used to the idea that she would do this in future. Then Barbara suddenly stopped making such arrangements without explaining why and waited for others to take over the reins of social secretary and to contact her about such arrangements. When they didn't (because they were waiting for her to take the lead as usual), she thought that she was being neglected by her friends and that, after all she had done for them, she didn't deserve such neglect. What Barbara failed to appreciate was her part in this 'neglect'.

Being unfairly excluded

Being unfairly excluded by a significant other when the person thinks they do not deserve to be is also a common inference in hurt, particularly in three-person situations where all are friends but two of the people have more in common than the third.

This happened to Felicity, who was friends with Gill and Tina and was the third person in this unbalanced triangle, in that Gill and Tina were closer with one another than they were with Felicity. In this situation, Felicity considered that she deserved to get equal attention from the two other people and that it was unfair for them to speak to each other for a lengthy period of time and exclude her.

Not being appreciated

Not being appreciated when the person considers that they deserve to be is another common inference made by them when they feel hurt. The person who makes this inference often disregards the reality of the situation, where the person from whom appreciation is expected is not known for showing it. Heather did a lot for her boss, who was particularly unappreciative. When he didn't show her appreciation for what she did for him, Heather made herself feel hurt about the unfairness of his unappreciative behaviour.

Being deprived of what one wants when one thinks one has deserved it

As you have now seen, the concept of deservingness is an important one in situations about which a person makes themselves feel hurt. This concept can be applied to any situation where the person has been deprived of what they want. If a person focuses on one of their relationships where they consider that they are not getting from the other what they deserve, they will feel hurt about this deprivation as long as they bring their hurt-creating rigid/extreme attitudes (see below) to this undeserved deprivation.

The person holds and rehearses rigid/extreme attitudes towards their inference

You have probably grasped one of the main points of this book by now, which is that in order to make themself feel emotionally disturbed about something, it is necessary for a person to hold a disturbance-creating rigid/extreme attitude towards this something. The corollary of this is that situations or the inferences that the person makes about situations, while contributing to their disturbed feelings, do not on their own disturb them. Rather, the person disturbs themself about these situations (actual or inferred) by their rigid/extreme attitudes. Applying this to the topic of hurt, we can say that being unfairly excluded, for example, does not make a person feel hurt; rather, the person makes themself feel hurt about unfair exclusion by the rigid/extreme attitudes that they hold about this actual or inferred event. Presently I will discuss what these rigid/extreme attitudes are.

Ego hurt and non-ego hurt

Before I do so, I want to make an important distinction between two types of hurt: ego hurt and non-ego hurt. When a person makes themself feel hurt in the ego domain, they feel hurt because they are devaluing themself in some way for the undeserved treatment they have experienced at the hands of a significant other. By contrast, when a person makes themself feel hurt in the non-ego domain, they are focusing on how horrible the world is for allowing them to be treated in such an unfair way. They are not devaluing themself for this treatment; rather, they feel sorry for themself for the way they have been treated. To complicate matters, as with unhealthy anger, it is possible for a person to make themself feel hurt in both ego and non-ego domains about the same event.

Now let me discuss the rigid/extreme attitudes that lead to hurt in both these domains. Let me begin with ego hurt.

RIGID/EXTREME ATTITUDES IN EGO HURT

To feel ego hurt a person needs at least two attitudes:

- A rigid demand (e.g. 'You must not reject me'); and
- A self-devaluation attitude (e.g. 'Your rejection makes me unlovable').

Sometimes when unhealthy anger is a feature of hurt, the person also holds an other-devaluation attitude (e.g. 'You are rotten for rejecting me since you are reminding me that I am unlovable').

RIGID/EXTREME ATTITUDES IN NON-EGO HURT

To feel non-ego hurt a person tends to hold:

- A rigid demand (e.g. 'You must not betray me') and one, two or all of the following extreme attitudes:
- An awfulising attitude (e.g. 'It is awful that you betrayed me. Poor me, I don't deserve to be treated like this');
- An unbearability attitude (e.g. 'I can't stand being betrayed. Poor me, I don't deserve to be treated like this');
- A world-devaluation attitude (e.g. 'The world is a rotten place for allowing such bad treatment to poor, undeserving me');
- An other-devaluation attitude (e.g. 'You are a bad person for betraying me'). This is particularly the case where unhealthy anger is a feature of non-ego hurt.

Thinking that stems from hurt-based rigid/extreme attitudes

As I have discussed with the other unhealthy negative emotions, when a person holds a hurt-creating rigid/extreme attitude towards any of the factors I discussed earlier in the chapter, this attitude will influence how they subsequently think in the following ways.

Overestimating the unfairness of the other person's behaviour

As I discussed earlier in this chapter, a person is much more likely to make themself feel hurt about being treated badly by those close to them when they consider that they do not deserve such treatment than when they think that they do deserve such treatment. When the person holds hurt-based rigid/extreme attitudes and when they think again about how they have been treated by the other person, their tendency is to overestimate the unfairness in the way they have been treated. Specifically, they may think about all the good things they have done for the other person and edit out all the good things that the other has done for them. Consequently, the person will dwell on the unfair imbalance that their rigid/extreme attitudes lead them to focus on.

Remember that this bias is a feature of the original inference about which the person made themself feel hurt, but it is more pronounced after being processed, as it were, by the person's hurt-based rigid/extreme attitudes.

Seeing the other person as showing lack of care or showing indifference

When a person holds hurt-based rigid/extreme attitudes towards the unfair treatment that they have experienced at the hands of someone close to them, they will tend to conclude that the reason why the other treated them so badly is because the other doesn't care about them or is indifferent to them. They will then tend to focus on that lack of caring or indifference and may well disturb themself about this stance by thinking in extreme ways about it.

Seeing oneself as alone, uncared for or misunderstood

When a person holds hurt-based rigid/extreme attitudes towards being mistreated by a significant other, they will tend to see themself placed in a negative situation in relation to the world. This view is usually an overgeneralisation. When a person is mistreated and makes themself feel hurt about it, they will tend to see themself as alone in the world, uncared for in the world or misunderstood by the world. This negative situation will be coloured by ego-based hurt (e.g. 'I am uncared for in the world; this proves that I am not worth caring about') or by non-ego-based hurt (e.g. 'I am alone in the world. Poor me!').

Thinking of past 'hurts'

When a person has made themself feel hurt by holding a relevant hurt-based rigid/extreme attitude, they tend to focus on past hurts. These 'hurts' may involve the other person about whom they currently feel hurt or may be broader and involve past 'hurts' with others in general. These 'hurts' may be similar in content to the specific incident the person currently feels hurt about (e.g. lack of appreciation) or they may be much broader and involve being mistreated, unappreciated, unfairly deprived, unfairly rejected by people.

Thinking that the other person has to put things right of their own accord

When I discuss sulking in the following section, I will point out that one of the purposes of such behaviour is to encourage the other person to take action of their own accord to put things right between them and the person who feels hurt and is sulking. Hurt-based rigid/extreme attitudes encourage the person to think this way. Here the person reminds themself that since they were unfairly treated (for example) by the other person, the fair thing for that person to do would be to make the first move. Thinking this way will also help to strengthen the person's conviction in their hurt-based rigid/extreme attitude.

Behaviour that stems from hurt-based rigid/extreme attitudes

When a person holds hurt-based rigid/extreme attitudes, they will tend to act in certain ways. When they do act in these ways, they rehearse and therefore strengthen their conviction in these rigid/extreme attitudes.

Blaming the other person for making them feel hurt

As with unhealthy anger, when discussing their feelings of hurt with friends and acquaintances, the person tends to place the blame for their hurt feelings on the behaviour of the person about whom they feel hurt. They do not take responsibility for their own feelings in this respect. This prevents the person from taking steps to deal with their hurt feelings by identifying and changing their hurt-based rigid/extreme attitudes.

Shutting down direct channels of communication with the other person while communicating indirectly that the other person has 'hurt' them

When the person holds hurt-based rigid/extreme attitudes, they tend to shut down direct channels of communication with the person about whom they feel hurt. The main point here is that the person does not tell the other what they feel hurt about; rather, they tend to *indirectly* show the other person how they feel. This is commonly known as sulking.

Sulking comes in two major forms. The first involves the person not talking to the other person at all. They can either do this loudly (e.g. by banging doors) or quietly (by silently rebuffing all attempts by the other person to engage them in direct communication). The second form of sulking involves the person criticising the other person but not telling that person what they feel hurt about.

As I showed in my book *The Incredible Sulk* (Sheldon Press, 1992), sulking has a number of purposes that serve to maintain the person's hurt-based rigid/extreme attitudes if acted on:

- To punish the other for 'hurting' their feelings.
- To get what they want from the other person.
- To get the other person to make the first move.
  (Part of the philosophy that underpins hurt is that the person has been treated unfairly by the other, whose responsibility it is to make efforts to find out how they have 'hurt' them and then to put things right between them. It is also part of this philosophy not to make this process too easy for the other person.)
- To extract proof of caring from the other person.
  (Here the other has to prove that they care about the person by making continued attempts to get them to talk. If they don't do this or give up too easily, the person has something else to make themselves feel hurt about.)
- To protect themselves from further hurt.
  (By doing this the person is practising their hurt-creating rigid/extreme attitude indirectly – it is as if they are saying: 'I need to stop communicating with this other person because if I continue to communicate with them, they will keep acting in ways that I will feel hurt about. Thus, I'll stop communicating.')
- To restore a sense of power.
  (Here sulking is an attempt by the person to get the upper hand in the relationship with the other who in their mind has 'hurt' them. In doing so, they reinforce their hurt-creating rigid/extreme attitudes.)

People develop and rehearse general hurt-based rigid/extreme attitudes

General hurt-based rigid/extreme attitudes are rigid/extreme attitudes that a person holds in many theme-related situations that result in them experiencing hurt in these situations. Developing and rehearsing such attitudes will lead the person to experience hurt in a variety of different situations. They will do this mainly because they tend to make inferences, for example, that those close to them do not appreciate them or have treated them unfairly.

Let me show you how this works. First, the person develops a general hurt-based rigid/extreme attitude (in this case in the non-ego domain) such as: 'Those close to me must include me in everything that they do and it's terrible if they don't. Poor me if I am excluded.' They then rehearse this general attitude until they firmly believe it and bring it to relevant situations where it is possible that others may not include them. Then, because they cannot convince themself that these others are willing to include them or that there is a good reason for their exclusion, they will tend to think that the others have unfairly excluded them and have done so intentionally. Having created this hurt-based inference, the person then brings a specific version of this general hurt-based rigid/extreme attitude to it and thereby makes themself feel hurt in the specific situation.

Let me give you a concrete example. Fay developed the following general hurt-based rigid/extreme attitude: 'Because I would not betray the trust of those close to me, they must not betray my trust and if they do, the world is a rotten place for allowing this to happen to poor, undeserving me.' She took this belief to a specific situation where she learned that her sister, whose confidences she had kept in the past, *may* have told a group of their mutual friends, when drunk, something that Fay told her in strict confidence. Fay's general hurt-based rigid/extreme attitude led her to infer that her sister did, in fact, betray her trust. It as if Fay reasoned: 'Because I can't convince myself that my sister did not betray my trust, then she did. If she did so, she betrayed my trust intentionally.' Fay's rigid/extreme attitude did not allow her to think that her sister did not betray her trust or that if she did, she did so unintentionally because she was drunk. Once Fay created this inference that she had been betrayed, she made herself feel hurt about it by holding a specific version of her general rigid/extreme attitude. Thus: 'My sister betrayed my trust intentionally by telling our mutual friends something that I told her in confidence. She absolutely should not have betrayed me and the world is a rotten place for allowing this to happen to poor, undeserving me.'

People develop and rehearse a view of the world founded on hurt-based rigid/extreme attitudes

The world views that render a person vulnerable to feelings of hurt do so, as I have pointed out throughout this book, primarily because they make it very easy for the person to make hurt-related inferences. Then the person makes themself feel hurt about these inferences with the appropriate rigid/extreme attitudes. Here is an illustrative list of the hurt-related world views that a person develops and the inferences that they spawn.

World view: When I do a lot for those close to me, they will fail to reciprocate.
Inference: People close to me will let me down.

World view: If I trust those close to me, they will often betray me, while I would not betray them.
Inference: People close to me will betray me.

World view: Significant others will act unfairly towards me, while I would not be unfair to them.
Inference: I will not get what I deserve from significant others.

World view: Those close to me will often exclude or neglect me for no good reason.
Inference: If I learn that people close to me are doing things with each other when I have not been invited, this is evidence that I have been excluded or neglected.

In the next chapter, I will discuss sorrow, the healthy alternative to hurt.

Further reading

Academic

Vangelisti, A. (Ed.) (2009). *Feeling hurt in close relationships.* New York: Cambridge University Press.

Self-help

Dryden, W. (2007). *Overcoming hurt.* London: Sheldon.

Chapter 12

Understanding sorrow

In this chapter, I will argue that sorrow is the healthy emotion alternative to hurt. As with some of the other healthy negative emotions, while the components of sorrow are clear, the term 'sorrow' has not been universally accepted as a plausible name for this emotion. Nevertheless, in this chapter, I will use this term.

The components of remorse

When a person feels sorrow:

1   They make certain types of inference.
2   They bring a set of sorrow-based flexible/non-extreme attitudes to those inferences.
3   They think in ways that are consistent with the above flexible/non-extreme attitudes.
4   They act in ways that are consistent with these flexible/non-extreme attitudes.
5   They rehearse a general version of their specific sorrow-based flexible/non-extreme attitudes which helps them to see the world more objectively than when they utilise and rehearse general hurt-based rigid and extreme attitudes.
6   They develop and rehearse a sorrow-based world view.

Now let me deal with these issues one at a time.

Inferences in sorrow

When a person experiences sorrow as a healthy alternative to hurt, they make the same inferences as they do when they experience

DOI: 10.4324/9781003203483-18

hurt. Again these inferences do not have to reflect accurately what is happening or what has happened. The important point is that person has to believe that they are true. In certain respects, the following inferences can be subsumed under the general heading 'I am more invested in our relationship than the other person is'. Here is a reminder of a list of these inferences:[1]

- Being unfairly criticised.
- Being rejected.
- Being disapproved by the other person.
- Being betrayed by the other.
- Being neglected.
- Being unfairly excluded.
- Not being appreciated.
- Being deprived of what one wants when one thinks one has deserved it.

The person holds and rehearses flexible/non-extreme attitudes towards their inference

As we have seen, at the core of healthy negative emotions, which are the healthy alternatives to emotional disturbance, the person holds a set of flexible/non-extreme attitudes towards the inferences that they make. In this context, a person will feel sorrow when they make one or more of the above inferences *and* when they hold flexible/non-extreme attitudes towards these inferences.

So let me discuss which flexible/non-extreme attitudes are at the root of sorrow.

Ego sorrow and non-ego sorrow

Before I do so, I want to make an important distinction between two types of sorrow: ego sorrow and non-ego sorrow. When a person feels sorrow in the ego domain, they accept themself unconditionally when they are treated in an undeserved way by a significant other. By contrast, when a person feels sorrow in the non-ego domain, they unconditionally accept the world but really don't like it when they are treated in such an unfair way.

Now let me discuss the flexible/non-extreme attitudes that lead to sorrow in both these domains. Let me begin with ego sorrow.

FLEXIBLE/NON-EXTREME ATTITUDES IN EGO SORROW

When a person feels ego sorrow, they hold at least two attitudes:

- A flexible attitude (e.g. 'I really don't want you to reject me, but that does not mean that you must not do so.'); and
- An unconditional self-acceptance attitude (e.g. 'Your rejection does not make me unlovable. I am a fallible human being able to be loved whether you accept me or reject me.')

FLEXIBLE/NON-EXTREME ATTITUDES IN NON-EGO SORROW

When a person feels non-ego sorrow they tend to hold:

- A flexible attitude (e.g. 'I would have much preferred you not to have betrayed me, but that does not mean that you must not do so.')
  and one, two or all of the following non-extreme attitudes:
- A non-awfulising attitude (e.g. 'It is bad that you betrayed me, but it is not awful. I am not "poor me" even though I am in a poor situation right now.')
- A bearability attitude (e.g. 'It is difficult for me to bear you betraying me, but I can bear it and it is worth it to me to do so. I am willing to bear it and I am going to do so. I am not "poor me" even though I am in a poor situation right now.')
- An unconditional world-acceptance attitude (e.g. 'The world is not a rotten place for allowing such bad treatment to happen to me. The world is a complex mixture of the good, the bad and the neutral.')
- An unconditional other-acceptance attitude (e.g. 'You are not a bad person for betraying me. You are a fallible human being who has acted badly on this occasion, but you also act well.')

Thinking that stems from sorrow-based flexible/non-extreme attitudes

As I have discussed with the other healthy negative emotions, when a person holds a sorrow-creating flexible/non-extreme attitude towards any of the factors I discussed earlier in the chapter, this attitude will influence how they subsequently think in the following ways.

Being realistic about the degree of unfairness in the other person's behaviour

As I discussed earlier in this chapter, a person experiences sorrow about being treated badly by those close to them when they consider that they do not deserve such treatment rather than when they think that they do deserve such treatment and crucially when they hold sorrow-based flexible/non-extreme attitudes. When this happens and when they think again about how they have been treated by the other person, they will be realistic about the degree of unfairness in the way they have been treated. While they may think about all the good things they have done for the other person, they will also acknowledge all the good things that the other has done for them.

Seeing the other person as acting badly rather than showing lack of care or showing indifference

When a person holds sorrow-based flexible/non-extreme attitudes towards the unfair treatment that they have experienced at the hands of someone close to them, they will not tend to conclude that the reason why the other treated them so badly is because the other doesn't care about them or is indifferent to them. Rather, they will think that the other's behaviour is motivated by a far less pernicious reason.

Seeing oneself as being in a poor situation but still connected to, cared for and understood by others not directly involved in the situation

When a person holds sorrow-based flexible/non-extreme attitudes towards being mistreated by a significant other, they will tend to see themself in a poor situation but not in relation to the world as a whole. Although in a poor situation, they will still tend to see themself connected to, cared for and understood by others not directly involved in the situation.

Thinking of past 'hurts', but with less frequency and less intensity than when holding hurt-based rigid/extreme attitudes

When a person holds a sorrow-based flexible/non-extreme attitude, they may still think about past hurts, but they will do so less frequently and less intensely than when holding hurt-based rigid/extreme attitudes.

Thinking that either person can make the first move to put things right

As I discussed in Chapter 11, when the person holds hurt-related attitudes, they tend to think that the other has to make the first move to put things right because the other is the one responsible for their 'hurt'. By contrast, when the person holds sorrow-based attitudes, while they may hope the other will make that first move, they are open to the possibility that they can make that move.

Behaviour that stems from sorrow-based flexible/non-extreme attitudes

When a person holds sorrow-based flexible/non-extreme attitudes, they will tend to act in certain ways.

Communicating one's feelings directly to the other

When the person holds sorrow-based flexible/non-extreme attitudes, they will keep open the channels of communication with the person who has acted badly towards them and tell them how they feel about the other's treatment of them. Contrast this with the sulking behaviour that the person engages in when they hold hurt-related attitudes.

Asserting oneself with the other and requesting change

When the person holds sorrow-based rather than hurt-based attitudes towards mistreatment from another, for example, the person will tend to assert themself with the other person and request change from that person.

While doing this, since the person takes responsibility for their own feelings, they will also take responsibility for any contribution they may have made to the situation which led to their mistreatment.

People develop and rehearse general sorrow-based flexible/non-extreme attitudes

General sorrow-based flexible/non-extreme attitudes are attitudes that a person holds in many theme-related situations that result in them experiencing sorrow rather than hurt in these situations. When they do this, they only make sorrow-related inferences when it is clear that such events have occurred. They will then evaluate such situations with specific variants of these general sorrow-based flexible/non-extreme attitudes.

People develop and rehearse a view of the world founded on sorrow-based flexible/non-extreme attitudes

I have made the point in previous chapters that people develop world views that render them vulnerable to or protect them from particular unhealthy negative emotions. The world views that underpin a person's tendency to experience sorrow rather than hurt are as follows, together with the inferences that they spawn.

World view: When I do a lot for those close to me, most will reciprocate, but some won't.
Inference: People close to me may let me down, but most of the time they won't.

World view: If I trust those close to me, some may betray me but certainly not all. I would not in general betray them, but I am not exempt from doing so.
Inference: People close to me may betray me, but they probably won't.

World view: Significant others may act unfairly towards me, but most won't. I would not, in general, be unfair to them, but I am not exempt from being so.
Inference: Most of the time, but not all the time, I will get what I deserve from significant others.

World view: Sometimes those close to me will exclude or neglect me for no good reason that I can see, but they will not do so often.
Inference: If I learn that people close to me are doing things with each other when I have not been invited, this may be evidence

that I have been excluded or neglected, but they may have had perfectly good reasons for their behaviour.

In the next chapter, I will discuss unhealthy jealousy.

Note

1 See Chapter 11 for a discussion of these inferences.

Part 7

Unhealthy jealousy and healthy jealousy

Chapter 13

Understanding unhealthy jealousy

Unhealthy jealousy ruins relationships! If a person has a problem with this type of jealousy, they will make it very difficult for anyone to have an ongoing loving relationship with them. In fact, in order for someone to sustain an ongoing relationship with the person, they will have to have the patience of a saint and either low self-esteem or an unhealthy need to help the person overcome their jealousy problem.

Before I discuss the nature of unhealthy jealousy, let me again discuss terminology. As with anger, we don't have very good words to discriminate between unhealthy and healthy jealousy, so I will use these two terms here. By *unhealthy (or problematic) jealousy*, I mean a state where a person demands that their partner must only have eyes for them and must not show interest in anyone they deem to be a love rival. The person's inclination is to monitor their partner closely for signs that they are interested in another person, question them closely to this effect and either check on their whereabouts or restrict their movements.

By contrast, *healthy (or non-problematic) jealousy* is a state where the person prefers that their partner only has eyes for them and does not show interest in anyone they deem to be a love rival, but does not insist that this must be the case. The person's inclination is to assume that their partner is not interested in another person unless they have clear evidence to the contrary and if they do, they will confront their partner with their evidence in a clear, assertive way. In general, the person will not monitor their partner closely for signs that they are interested in another person, question them closely to this effect, check on their whereabouts or restrict their movements.

The components of unhealthy jealousy

Below I list the components of unhealthy jealousy:

1. The person makes certain types of inference.
2. They bring a set of unhealthy jealousy-based rigid/extreme attitudes to those inferences.
3. They think in ways that are consistent with the above rigid/extreme attitudes.
4. They act in ways that are consistent with these rigid/extreme attitudes.
5. They rehearse a general version of their specific unhealthy jealousy-based rigid/extreme attitudes so that they are prone to make certain threat-related inferences with respect to their relationship.
6. They develop and rehearse a unhealthy jealousy-based world view.

I will now deal with these issues one at a time. As I do, I will concentrate on unhealthy romantic jealousy.

Inferences in unhealthy jealousy

To feel unhealthy jealous, a person needs first to focus on a scenario (which can be real or imagined) that has three people in it: the person, their partner (a term that I use broadly here) and another person whom the person views as an actual or potential love rival. Then the person makes an inference that the other person poses a threat to their relationship with their partner. The nature of this threat is likely to be fivefold. A person may make one or more of these inferences.

'My partner will leave me'

The person regards the other person in the triangle as someone who will replace them in the affections of their partner and thinks that their partner will leave them for the other person.

'I'm not the most important person in my partner's life'

The person thinks that their partner finds the other person more attractive than them and that they will be displaced as the most important person in their partner's life (even though they do not think that their partner will go off with the other person).

'I'm not my partner's "one and only"'

The person acknowledges that it is important to them that their partner is only interested in them and that their partner's interest in the other person means that they are no longer the partner's 'one and only'.

'Someone is showing an interest in my partner'

The person acknowledges that it is important to them that no one (who has the potential to be a love rival) shows an interest in their partner, so when someone does, they deem this to be a threat.

'I don't know what my partner is doing or thinking'

Here the person realises that unless they place their partner under constant surveillance (which they may well like to do!), they will not know what their partner is doing. Indeed, even if they do manage to know at all times what their partner is doing, it is unlikely that they will ever know for sure what they are thinking. Thus, uncertainty about one's partner is a key inference in unhealthy jealousy

As I have mentioned several times in this book, these inferences don't have to reflect accurately what is happening or what has happened. In fact, when a person is feeling unhealthy jealousy, their inferences are likely to be false. The important point is that *they* think that they are true.

The person holds and rehearses rigid/extreme attitudes towards their inference(s)

You will by now not need reminding that a person's unhealthy jealousy is not caused by their inference that their partner may find another person attractive, for example. Rather, these unhealthy feelings are largely determined by the rigid/extreme attitudes that the person holds towards this inference, true or not.

Let me discuss these points with reference to Sylvia, who was uncertain about what her partner was doing at his office party, to which she had not been invited. She brought the following rigid/

extreme attitudes to this uncertainty, which were in the area of non-ego disturbance (where the person's problem was not related to her view of herself):

- A rigid demand (e.g. 'I must know that my partner does not find anyone at the party attractive').
- An unbearability attitude (e.g. 'I can't stand not knowing that my partner does not find anyone at the party attractive').

As I will discuss later in the chapter, these unhealthy jealousy-based rigid/extreme attitudes led Sylvia to conclude that under these circumstances her partner did find other women at the party attractive and that, for example, this meant that she was not the one and only person that he finds attractive. Then she focused on this situation and held the following rigid/extreme attitudes (which were in the area of ego disturbance, where she devalued herself in some way):

- A rigid demand (e.g. 'My partner must find only me attractive').
- A self-devaluation attitude (e.g. 'If my partner finds other women attractive, this means that I am unattractive and worthless').

Here are similar rigid/extreme attitudes towards the other inferences I discussed earlier. Thus:

- 'My partner must not leave me. If they do, it proves that I am unlovable.'
- 'I must be the most important person in my partner's life. If I'm not, then I am nothing.'
- 'I must be my partner's one and only. If I am not, then I am worthless.'

The above rigid/extreme attitudes exemplify ego disturbance.

When a person holds rigid/extreme attitudes towards other people showing an interest in their partner and the basis of the person's disturbance does not concern their view of themself (i.e. non-ego disturbance), the following are found:

- 'Nobody else must show an interest in my partner. If they do, it's terrible.'
- 'Nobody else must show an interest in my partner. If they do, I couldn't bear it.'

- 'Nobody else must show an interest in my partner. If they do, they are no good.'

Thinking that stems from unhealthy jealousy-based rigid/extreme attitudes

When a person holds a unhealthy jealousy-based rigid/extreme attitude towards any of the inferences I discussed earlier in the chapter, this attitude will influence the ways in which they subsequently think about relevant aspects of the total situation. Here are some common examples of such subsequent thinking.

Distrusting and being suspicious of one's partner

When a person holds attitudes that underpin unhealthy jealousy and they experience this emotion, they tend to think that whatever their partner says or does, they are not to be trusted. In this frame of mind, the person looks for discrepancies in what their partner says and/or does. This will be particularly the case when they keep note of their partner's movements, which provides them with what they consider to be the necessary ammunition. When the person finds a discrepancy, however small, they tend to remind themself that this is evidence that their partner cannot be trusted.

Thinking of relevant people as love rivals

When a person holds attitudes that underpin unhealthy jealousy and they experience this emotion in one context, they can unwittingly maintain their jealousy problem by thinking that relevant people (deemed by the person to be attractive) are potential love rivals. Doing this results in the person inferring that their relationship with their partner is always under threat – one of the main features of a chronic unhealthy jealousy problem.

Thinking that one's partner has a negative attitude towards one

The person's unhealthy jealousy-related rigid/extreme attitudes will lead them to think that their partner has a negative attitude towards them. They will then tend to think of all the negative things that their partner has said about them. This will reinforce the person's self-devaluation attitude that they are not worth caring about.

Thinking in distorted ways about one's partner's behaviour

Once a person holds unhealthy jealousy-based attitudes towards their partner's behaviour (for example, talking to an attractive person at a social gathering), they tend to think in negatively distorted ways about their partner's behaviour, which serves to maintain their unhealthy jealousy feelings. Thus, in the above example, the person will tend to think one or more of the following:

- 'My partner wants to have an affair with the other person.'
- 'My partner is betraying me.'
- 'My partner is rejecting me.'
- 'My partner is making me look a fool in the eyes of other people.'

Thinking in such distorted ways will increase the chances that the person will perpetuate their unhealthy jealousy feelings, particularly if they hold rigid/extreme attitudes towards these distortions (e.g. 'By talking to that person, which they must not do, my partner is rejecting me and this proves that I am worthless').

Thinking in distorted ways about one's future relationships

Once a person holds unhealthy jealousy-based attitudes towards their present relationship, and these have been activated, then the person will also tend to think in negatively distorted ways about potential future relationships. Thus, when the person feels unhealthy jealousy about their partner's unfaithful behaviour (real or more likely imagined), for example, they think that any future partners they might have will also act in the same ways and that they will never have a relationship with someone who will be faithful to them.

Thinking negatively about one's own qualities (particularly in relation to possible love rivals)

When the person's unhealthy jealousy-related attitudes have been activated and they experience this emotion, they tend to think negatively about their own qualities. Thus, when Linda felt unhealthy jealousy about her partner talking to an attractive woman, she thought that, by comparison, she was unattractive, uninteresting and unintelligent. These negative thoughts will tend to fuel her self-devaluation attitude and thus increase the chances that she will experience unhealthy jealousy in the future.

Thinking positively about the qualities of one's love rivals (particularly in relation to oneself)

The counterpart to thinking negatively about themself when the person's unhealthy jealousy-based attitude has been activated is thinking positively about the qualities of potential love rivals. Thus, when Sylvia experienced unhealthy jealousy about her partner talking to an attractive woman, she thought that, in comparison to her, the other woman was attractive, interesting and intelligent. These thoughts will again help fuel her self-devaluation attitude and thus increase the chances that she will experience unhealthy jealousy in the future.

Like a lot of people with a jealousy problem, Sylvia combined thinking negatively about herself with thinking positively about her love rival. In doing so, she doubled the chances that she would make herself unhealthily jealous in the future.

Behaviour that stems from unhealthy jealousy-based rigid/extreme attitudes

When a person holds unhealthy jealousy-based rigid/extreme attitudes, they will tend to act in certain ways. When they do act in these ways, they rehearse and therefore strengthen their conviction in these rigid/extreme attitudes.

Seeking constant reassurance that one is loved (but never truly believing it)

The rigid/extreme attitudes that underpin unhealthy jealousy lead the person to 'feel' unloved. In order to escape this 'feeling', the person experiencing unhealthy jealousy seeks reassurance that their partner loves them and does this constantly, but without really being convinced of the answers that they get. Their partner tends to reinforce this behaviour by providing intermittent reinforcement – sometimes responding that they love the person and sometimes not.

Questioning one's partner constantly, but not accepting what the partner says

The person's unhealthy jealousy-based rigid/extreme attitudes will lead them to question their partner about their feelings, thoughts and behaviours, particularly with respect to any potential love rivals. When their partner answers such questions, the person tends not to believe the veracity of the partner's responses. They will look for any inconsistencies in what their partner says and ask further questions about these inconsistencies.

If their partner refuses to answer their questions, the person may well accuse their partner of being unfaithful to them. When their partner denies these accusations, the person will take what the partner says and ask further questions. The person may well keep this process going until their partner storms off. When the person next sees their partner, they may also tell the partner that their storming off is proof that they have been unfaithful to them.

Checking on one's partner constantly

When the person is not in their partner's presence, their unhealthy jealousy-related rigid/extreme attitudes will lead them to make checks on their partner. There are several ways in which the person can do this. Thus, they can:

- Follow their partner surreptitiously.
- Phone or text their partner.
- Get reports on their partner's activities from friends. If the person is wealthy, they may even hire a private investigator.

The person's checking behaviours will have the effect of maintaining their unhealthy jealousy by keeping in their mind that there is a threat to their relationship with their partner and, if they don't know what their partner is doing, for example, then that proves that the latter is 'up to no good'. Having constructed these thoughts, the person may well hold rigid/extreme attitudes towards them, thus entrenching their jealousy problem.

Monitoring one's partner closely when in their presence

When a person is with their partner, their unhealthy jealousy-based rigid/extreme attitudes will lead them to monitor their partner closely, particularly when in the presence of potential love rivals. These rigid/extreme attitudes will also encourage the person to assume that their partner is looking at one such rival if the person sees their partner glancing in the rival's general direction and to further assume that their partner is interested in the rival. Such monitoring will keep the idea in the person's mind that threats to their relationship with their partner are everywhere, a key component of unhealthy jealousy.

The person may also tend to monitor the behaviour and gaze direction of their potential love rivals and assume that they are interested in their partner even in the absence of corroborating evidence.

Accusing one's partner of indiscretions and infidelities

A person's unhealthy jealousy-related rigid/extreme attitudes will also encourage them to accuse their partner of various indiscretions and infidelities. If they do this frequently, their partner may well eventually withdraw from them because their partner finds the person's behaviour aversive. The person will then take their partner's withdrawal as evidence that they are interested in someone else. The person will then accuse their partner of this and doing so will again increase their conviction that threats to their relationship are ubiquitous. They will, in all probability, then bring their rigid/extreme attitudes to this conclusion, which has the effect of deepening their unhealthy jealousy.

Setting traps for one's partner

One of my clients who had a problem with unhealthy jealousy suspected that her husband was interested in other women. So, at a works party she introduced him to an attractive woman whom she knew delighted in sleeping with other women's husbands. She then left the party, claiming to have a migraine, but insisted that her husband stay and give the woman a lift home. When he came home, she accused him of sleeping with the woman, even though he had neither the time nor the interest in doing so. In short, my client's unhealthy jealousy-based rigid/extreme attitudes led her to set a trap for her husband. This only served to reinforce my client's rigid/extreme attitudes.

It is clear, then, that setting traps for one's partner will serve to perpetuate a person's unhealthy jealousy and have a very negative impact on their relationship. If a person sets such traps for their partner frequently, their partner may leave them. While the person will then conclude that they were right all along about their partner's interest in other people, the reality is that the person's own behaviour served to make their relationship unsustainable from their partner's point of view. Sadly, when in the grip of unhealthy jealousy, the person is so blinkered that they cannot see what is obvious to others.

Placing restrictions on one's partner

When a person holds unhealthy jealousy-based rigid/extreme attitudes, doing so will lead them to place restrictions on their partner that effectively stop them engaging in activities that *the person* finds threatening. For example, Laragh feared that her partner would talk to and show interest in potential love rivals at social gatherings to which she had not been invited and thus banned her partner from attending these functions. In doing so, she reinforced her unhealthy jealousy because, by placing restrictions on her partner, she was acting on the following ideas: 'I forbid you to attend social gatherings without me because:

- If you go, I will not know what you are getting up to and I need to know that you are not showing interest in a potential love rival because if I don't know this, I will assume that you are showing a romantic interest in this person'
and
- If you do talk to someone that I deem to be a love rival, this means that you prefer them to me and I couldn't stand that.'

Retaliating

Another way that the person acts on and thereby reinforces their unhealthy jealousy and the rigid/extreme attitudes that underpin it is by retaliating against their partner's presumed infidelities. I say 'presumed' here because the person may have little actual evidence that their partner has been unfaithful to them. When under the influence of their unhealthy jealousy-related attitudes, the person is not really concerned with actual evidence because they are convinced that their partner has been unfaithful. Given this, their rigid/extreme attitudes lead them to be unfaithful themself as a way of getting back at their partner. The person might even get their retaliation in first and have an affair before they discover that their partner has been unfaithful to them. After all, the person reasons, it is only a matter of time before they do.

Retaliating against their partner (before or after the event) serves to keep at the forefront of the person's mind the notion that there is an ever-present threat to their relationship, to which she will easily bring her rigid/extreme attitudes to create and perpetuate ever-present unhealthy jealousy.

Punishing one's partner

Retaliation helps to perpetuate unhealthy jealousy in that inherent in the idea of retaliating against one's partner is the inference that they have been unfaithful to the person (or will inevitably be so in the future). When the person punishes their partner, they also assume that the other already has been unfaithful to them in some way, thus strengthening the idea in their mind that threats to their relationship are ubiquitous, a conclusion to which they bring their rigid/extreme attitudes. Such punishments are particularly potent when the person does not disclose why they are punishing their partner. Here you will notice some overlap between unhealthy anger (see Chapter 9), unhealthy jealousy and feelings of hurt (see Chapter 11), particularly when the person punishes their partner by refusing to communicate with them (i.e. punishment by sulking). Another way of punishing one's partner for being unfaithful is for the person to berate their partner verbally. This is common when the person also clings to the notion that anything their partner may say in their defence is a lie!

Punishing one's love rival

Punishing a rival for taking one's partner away from one (for this is how the person inaccurately sees it in their mind) is another behaviour that stems from the person's unhealthy jealousy-based rigid/ extreme attitudes and serves to keep their unhealthy jealousy alive. It is important to recognise that when the person's unhealthy jealousy is chronic, such punishment frequently happens when there is no evidence at all that the rival has taken the partner from the person. The 'evidence' is all in the person's imagination. Exacting such punishment also serves to keep in the person's mind the notion that rivals to their partner's affections are omnipresent and are likely to be successful and thus gives the person a further opportunity to rehearse their unhealthy jealousy-related rigid/extreme attitudes, which they easily bring to such inferences.

People develop and rehearse general unhealthy jealousy-based rigid/extreme attitudes

General unhealthy jealousy-based rigid/extreme attitudes are rigid/extreme attitudes that a person holds in many theme-related situations that enable them to experience unhealthy jealousy in these situations. Developing and rehearsing such attitudes will enable the person to experience unhealthy jealousy in many different situations. They will do this mainly because they make frequent inferences that they are facing a threat to their relationship with their partner in the absence of corroborative evidence.

Let me show you how this works. First, the person needs to develop a general unhealthy jealousy-based rigid/extreme attitude such as: 'My partner must only show interest in me and if they show interest in someone else, it means that I am unworthy.' The person rehearses this general attitude until they have strong conviction in it and brings it to relevant situations where it is possible that their partner may show interest in someone else. Then, because the person cannot convince themself that their partner is not interested in the other person, they will tend to think that they are so interested and furthermore that the other person is interested in their partner and that they want to begin a relationship with one another. Having created this unhealthy jealousy-based inference, the person then brings a specific version of this general unhealthy jealousy-based rigid/extreme attitude to it and thereby makes themself feel unhealthily jealous in the specific situation.

Let me give you a concrete example of how this unfolds. Samantha developed the following general unhealthy jealousy-based rigid/extreme attitude: 'I must know at all times what my partner is doing and it's terrible if I don't know this.' She took this attitude to a specific situation where her partner left a message on her voicemail saying that he would be home late from work. Her general unhealthy jealousy-based rigid/extreme attitude led her to infer that her partner was out with a potential love rival. It is as if Samantha reasoned: 'Because I don't know what my partner is doing and it is terrible not to know, not knowing means that he is with someone else.' Her rigid/extreme attitude did not readily allow her to think that her partner was doing something completely innocent like working late on his own. Once

Samantha created her inference that her partner was with a love rival, it was fairly easy for her to make herself feel unhealthily jealous and bring the following specific unhealthy jealousy-based rigid/extreme attitude to it: 'My partner is with someone else tonight. He must not do this and because he is, it proves that I am worthless.'

Samantha then acted according to this rigid/extreme attitude and when her partner came home, she accused him of meeting a woman and verbally berated him when he denied this.

People develop and rehearse a view of the world founded on unhealthy jealousy-based rigid/extreme attitudes

The world views that render a person vulnerable to unhealthy jealousy do so again because they make it very easy for the person to make unhealthy jealousy-related inferences. Then, as I have shown you earlier in the chapter, they make themself unhealthily jealous about these inferences with the appropriate rigid/extreme attitudes. Here is an illustrative list of unhealthy jealousy-related world views and the inferences that they spawn.

World view: Partners will ultimately leave.
Inference: My partner is on the lookout for someone better.

World view: Partners are basically untrustworthy.
Inference: Whatever my partner says about their feelings towards me and love rivals is not to be taken at face value.

World view: If I trust someone, they will make a fool of me. So, I need to always be on my guard.
Inference: When my partner asks me to trust them, they are up to no good.

World view: Not knowing what partners are feeling, thinking and doing is very dangerous.
Inference: If I don't know what my partner is feeling, thinking or doing, this means that they are interested in someone else and/or they are thinking of leaving me.

In the next chapter, I will discuss healthy jealousy, which I deem to be the healthy alternative to unhealthy jealousy, especially when the threat to a person's relationship is clear and present.

Further reading

Academic

Salovey, P. (Ed.) (1991). *The psychology of jealousy and envy.* New York: Guilford.

Self-help

Dryden, W. (1998). *Overcoming jealousy.* London: Sheldon.

Chapter 14

Understanding healthy jealousy

I have made the point several times in this book that naming healthy negative emotions is fraught with difficulty. So, while the components of healthy jealousy are clear, the term 'healthy jealousy', as you will see, has not been universally accepted as a plausible name for this emotion. Some have called it non-problematic jealousy (as opposed to problematic jealousy) and others have called it good jealousy (as opposed to bad jealousy). Some have even refrained from using the term 'jealousy' altogether calling the healthy form of jealousy 'concern for one's relationship'. However, in this chapter the term I will use is 'healthy jealousy'.

The components of healthy jealousy

When a person experiences healthy jealousy:

1. They make certain types of inference.
2. They bring a set of healthy jealousy-based flexible/non-extreme attitudes to those inferences.
3. They think in ways that are consistent with the above flexible/non-extreme attitudes.
4. They act in ways that are consistent with these flexible/non-extreme attitudes.
5. They rehearse a general version of their specific healthy jealousy-based flexible/non-extreme attitudes which helps them to see the world more objectively than when they utilise and rehearse general unhealthy jealousy-based rigid and extreme attitudes.
6. They develop and rehearse a healthy jealousy-based world view.

Now let me deal with these issues one at a time.

Inferences in healthy jealousy

When a person experiences healthy jealousy as a healthy alternative to unhealthy jealousy, they make the same inferences as they do when they experience unhealthy jealousy. While these inferences do not have to reflect accurately what is happening or what has happened, they are more like to reflect that reality in healthy jealousy than in unhealthy jealousy, where the person makes inferences that objectively are unlikely to be true but are strongly experienced by the person as a true reflection of what is going on in their relationship. Here is a reminder of a list of these inferences:[1]

- 'My partner will leave me.'
- 'I'm not the most important person in my partner's life.'
- 'I'm not my partner's "one and only".'
- 'Someone is showing an interest in my partner.'
- 'I don't know what my partner is doing or thinking.'

The person holds flexible/non-extreme attitudes towards their inference(s)

As we have seen, at the core of healthy negative emotions, which are the healthy alternatives to emotional disturbance, the person holds a set of flexible/non-extreme attitudes towards the inferences that they make. In this context, a person will feel healthy jealousy when they make one or more of the above inferences *and* when they hold flexible/non-extreme attitudes towards these inferences.

So let me discuss which flexible/non-extreme attitudes are at the root of healthy jealousy. I will do so by reconsidering the case of Sylvia, whom we met in the previous chapter. Here she experiences healthy jealousy. If you recall, Sylvia was uncertain about what her partner was doing at his office party, to which she had not been invited. She brought the following flexible/non-extreme attitudes to this uncertainty:

- A flexible attitude (e.g. 'I would like to know that my partner does not find anyone at the party attractive, but I don't need to know this').
- A bearability attitude (e.g. 'It's a struggle for me not to know that my partner does not find anyone at the party attractive, but I can stand not knowing. It is worth it to me to bear this, I am willing to do so and I am going to do so.').

Understanding healthy jealousy

If Sylvia discovered that her partner did, in reality, find other women at the party attractive and that this meant that she was not the one and only person that he finds attractive, then her jealousy would be healthy if she held the following flexible/non-extreme attitudes:

- A flexible attitude (e.g. 'I want my partner to find only me attractive, but this does not have to be the case').
- An unconditional self-acceptance attitude (e.g. 'If my partner finds other women attractive, this does not mean that I am unattractive and worthless. My attractiveness and worth are fixed and not dependent on whether or not my partner finds other people attractive.').

Here are similar flexible/non-extreme attitudes towards the other inferences I discussed earlier. Thus:

- 'I really don't want my partner to leave me, but sadly this does not mean that they must not do so. If they do, it does not prove that I am unlovable. I am lovable whether or not my partner leaves me.'
- 'I would like to be the most important person in my partner's life, but it does not follow that I must be. I am the same fallible, worthwhile person no matter how important I am to my partner.'
- 'I very much want to be my partner's one and only, but I don't have to be. If I am not, then I can still accept myself as a unique, fallible person. I am certainly not worthless.'

The above flexible/non-extreme attitudes exemplify ego health.

When a person holds a flexible/non-extreme attitude towards other people showing an interest in their partner and the basis of the person's response does not concern their view of themselves (i.e. non-ego health), the following attitudes are found:

- 'I don't want anybody to show an interest in my partner, but it does not have to be that way. If they do, it's bad but not terrible.'
- 'I don't want anybody to show an interest in my partner, but it does not have to be that way. If they do, it would be hard to bear, but I could bear it. It's worth bearing, I am willing to bear it and I am going to bear it.'

- 'I don't want anybody to show an interest in my partner, but it does not have to be that way. If they do, that would be bad, but they are fallible humans and not worthless.'

Thinking that stems from healthy jealousy-based flexible/non-extreme attitudes

When a person holds a healthy jealousy-based flexible/non-extreme attitude towards any of the inferences I discussed earlier in the chapter, this attitude will influence the ways in which they subsequently think about relevant aspects of the total situation. Here are some common examples of such subsequent thinking.

Being realistic about any threat to one's relationship that does exist

Holding healthy jealousy-based attitudes leads the person to reflect on the threat that exists to their relationship and to see it realistically based on the facts of the matter.

Not misconstruing ordinary conversations between one's partner and another person

Holding healthy jealousy-based attitudes leads the person to reflect on conversations between their partner and another person who could be a love rival and to see them realistically rather than misconstruing them.

Accepting that your partner will find others attractive but not seeing this as a threat

Holding healthy jealousy-based attitudes leads the person to rethink the fact that their partner finds other people attractive and to see it as unfortunate but not necessarily a threat to their relationship.

Behaviour that stems from healthy jealousy-based flexible/non-extreme attitudes

When a person holds healthy jealousy-based flexible/non-extreme attitudes, they will tend to act in certain ways which tend to be constructive.

Allowing one's partner to initiate expressing love for one without prompting them or seeking reassurance once they have done so

The flexible and non-extreme attitudes that underpin healthy jealousy lead the person to wait for their partner to express love for the person of their own accord without seeking reassurance on this score. Because the person considers themself lovable, whether or not they are facing a threat to their relationship, they are able to wait for this to happen. The person is more likely to believe that their partner loves them when such love is spontaneously expressed than when it is expressed in response to the partner feeling under pressure to say it when the person, under the influence of unhealthy jealousy, is constantly asking if they are loved.

Allowing one's partner freedom without monitoring their feelings, actions and whereabouts

When the person's attitudes are flexible and non-extreme towards the possibility of there being a threat to their relationship, we have seen that the person is only likely to see a threat when it is clear that one exists. In the absence of such evidence, the attitudes that underpin healthy jealousy lead the person to allow their partner the freedom to think, feel and go where they please without monitoring them in any of these respects.

Allowing one's partner to show friendly interest in attractive people without setting tests

Again, because the person's attitudes in healthy jealousy are flexible and non-extreme towards the possibility of the existence of a relationship threat and because they only get jealous when such a threat is clear and present, the person allows their partner to talk and show friendly interest to all with whom they come into contact. They can do this because they are not threatened by the friendly interest that their partner may take even in those whom they may find attractive. The person can do this because they do not confuse attraction with action. They recognise that their partner may find someone attractive without wanting to do anything about it.

Communicating one's concern for one's relationship in an open and non-blaming manner

If the person does have clear evidence that there is a threat to their relationship with their partner posed by their partner's interest in someone else, their healthy jealousy attitudes lead the person to do the following. They express their concern for their relationship in ways that are clear and open and without blaming their partner. They can present their evidence in a descriptive manner and invite a response from their partner, to whom they give a fair hearing. Finally, they request that their partner change their behaviour to remove the threat to their relationship but do so without demanding that such change occurs. If the threat continues to exist after several such episodes, the person will begin to reappraise the viability of their relationship, ending it if the person concludes that it is no longer viable.

People develop and rehearse general healthy jealousy-based flexible/non-extreme attitudes

General healthy jealousy-based flexible/non-extreme attitudes are attitudes that a person holds in many theme-related situations that enable them to experience healthy jealousy in these situations. Developing and rehearsing such attitudes will enable the person to experience healthy jealousy in many different situations, but only when the threat to their relationship is clear and present. When it is not clear and present, then the person assumes that such a threat does not exist and therefore they will not experience jealousy.

People develop and rehearse a view of the world founded on healthy jealousy-based flexible/non-extreme attitudes

As previously discussed, people develop world views that render them vulnerable to or protect them from particular unhealthy negative emotions. The world views that underpin a person's tendency to experience healthy jealousy rather than unhealthy jealousy are as follows, together with the inferences that they spawn.

World view: Partners may leave, but they are more likely to stay.
Inference: My partner may be on the lookout for someone better, but they are probably not.

World view: Partners may be untrustworthy, but they are more likely to be trustworthy unless there is clear evidence to the contrary.
Inference: Whatever my partner says about their feelings towards me and love rivals can be taken at face value, unless I have clear evidence to the contrary.

World view: If I trust someone, they may make a fool of me, but it is more likely that they will not do this. So, I need to be careful, but not always on my guard.
Inference: When my partner asks me to trust them, I can probably do so, unless I have clear evidence that they are up to no good.

World view: Not knowing what partner are feeling, thinking and doing may be uncomfortable, but it certainly is not unbearable.
Inference: If I don't know what my partner is feeling, thinking or doing, this may mean that they are interested in someone else and/or they are thinking of leaving me, but without any clear corroborating evidence this is very unlikely.

In the next chapter, I will discuss unhealthy envy. This emotion often gets confused with unhealthy jealousy, but as you will see they are very different unhealthy negative emotions.

Note

1 See Chapter 13 for a discussion of these inferences.

Part 8

Unhealthy envy and healthy envy

Chapter 15

Understanding unhealthy envy

Unhealthy envy is a particularly destructive emotion. It can sour relationships and lead a person to become obsessed with what they don't have in life, leaving them to take for granted or neglect what they do have in life. As we will see, it can also lead a person to destroy or spoil what others have.

Before I discuss the nature of unhealthy envy, I need once again to discuss terminology. As with anger and jealousy, we don't have very good words to discriminate between unhealthy envy and healthy envy, so I will use these two terms here. By *unhealthy (or problematic) envy*, I mean a state where a person demands that they must have what they covet in others' lives. Their inclination is to aim to get what they lack at all costs or, if not, to spoil or destroy things for others. By contrast, *healthy (or non-problematic) envy* is a state where the person would like to have what they covet in others' lives but does not demand that they must get it. Their inclination is to strive for what they want as long as it is constructive to do so, and they experience little or no desire to spoil or destroy things for others.

The components of unhealthy envy

Below I list the components of unhealthy envy.

1 The person makes certain types of inference.
2 They bring a set of unhealthy envy-based rigid/extreme attitudes to those inferences.
3 They think in ways that are consistent with the above rigid/extreme attitudes.
4 They act in ways that are consistent with these rigid/extreme attitudes.

DOI: 10.4324/9781003203483-23

5   They rehearse a general version of their specific unhealthy envy-based rigid/extreme attitudes so that they easily tend to make inferences associated with envy.
6   They develop and rehearse a unhealthy envy-based world view.

I will now deal with these issues one at a time.

Inference in unhealthy envy

When a person feels unhealthy envy, they focus on a scenario (which can be real or imagined) that has three elements to it, usually: the person themself, another person (or people) and something or someone that the other has that the person prizes but does not have. When the person is envious, they are envious of *the presumed fact that someone has someone or something in their life that they do not have in their own life, but which they prize and desire*. This is the main inference in envy.

Envy is often confused with jealousy, which, as I showed in the previous chapters, involves the person thinking that they face a threat to their relationship with their partner. I often explain the difference in the following way. I am bald and I would like to have a full head of hair. Now, imagine that I meet a man with a full head of hair. If I were envious of the person's hair, I would be saying that I would like a full head of hair like the other person. If I were jealous of the person's hair, I would be saying that I think the person's hair (not the person himself) poses a threat to my relationship with my partner – clearly a ridiculous notion.

Here are several envy scenarios to show the range of things of which a person can be envious.

- Barry was envious of his friend's attractive wife (object of envy: a person).
- Linda was envious of her friend's good looks (object of envy: physical characteristics).
- Muriel was envious of her married friends' family life (object of envy: family life).
- Phil was envious of his friend's promotion (object of envy: achievement).
- Mr and Mrs Smith were envious of their friends' lavish lifestyle (object of envy: lifestyle).

- Ben was envious of his friend's extroversion (object of envy: personal characteristic).
- Jane was envious of Beryl's ability to play the piano (object of envy: talent).
- Bill was envious of his friend's Porsche (object of envy: possession).

As I have mentioned several times before in this book, these inferences do not have to reflect reality. The important point is that the person thinks that they are true.

The person holds and rehearses rigid/extreme attitudes towards the inference

Once again, I want to stress that a person's unhealthy envy is not caused by their inference that another person has something (or someone) that they want but do not have. Rather, these unhealthy feelings are largely determined by the rigid/extreme attitudes that the person holds towards this inference, true or not.

There are, in fact, two different types of unhealthy envy: unhealthy ego envy and unhealthy non-ego envy, although a person may have both.

Unhealthy ego envy

In unhealthy ego envy, the person tends to invest their self-esteem in whatever it is that others have that they want but don't have. When the person experiences unhealthy envy in the ego domain, they need to hold two rigid/extreme attitudes:

- A rigid demand (e.g. 'A colleague got promoted and I absolutely should get promoted as well').
- A self-devaluation attitude (e.g. 'I am less worthy than my colleague for not getting promoted').

Unhealthy non-ego envy

In unhealthy non-ego envy, the person disturbs themself about not having what they want, but they do not invest their self-esteem in whatever they don't have. They are more focused on their sense of non-ego deprivation. When the person experiences unhealthy envy in the non-ego domain, they need to hold two rigid/extreme attitudes:

- A rigid demand (e.g. 'A colleague got promoted and I absolutely should get promoted as well').
- An unbearability attitude (e.g. 'I can't stand the situation where my colleague got promoted and I didn't').

The importance of focus in unhealthy envy and the role of rigid/extreme attitudes

So far I have concentrated on discussing unhealthy envy where the focus is on the person wanting what someone else has and they do not have and then bringing a set of rigid/extreme attitudes to this situation. The person can also change the focus so that they want the other person not to have what they do not have, and then they make themself unhealthily envious when this desire is not met. Let's take the example I have just discussed, where a work colleague has been promoted and the person hasn't. I have shown how the person can make themself unhealthily envious by demanding: 'I must get promoted like my colleague.' But they can also make themself unhealthily envious by changing the focus of the situation so that they believe: 'My colleague absolutely should not have been promoted when I wasn't.' Note that, in both foci, it is the rigid/extreme attitudes that lead to unhealthy envy and not the focus itself.

The role of rigid/extreme attitudes in unhealthy envy: The examples revisited

Let me now illustrate the above by returning to the examples I outlined earlier. I will assume that in all the scenarios the envy experienced was unhealthy in nature.

- Barry was unhealthily envious of his friend's attractive wife (object of envy: a person).
  Barry's unhealthy envy was largely non-ego in nature. He thus held the following rigid/extreme attitudes: 'I must have an attractive wife like my friend has and I can't stand not having one.'
- Linda was unhealthily envious of her friend's good looks (object of envy: physical characteristics).
  Linda's unhealthy envy was largely ego in nature. She held the following rigid/extreme attitudes: 'I must be as attractive as my friend and I am less worthy than her because I am not.'

[This example shows the comparative aspect of envy as Linda is judging herself to be less worthy than her friend because she considers herself to be less attractive than her.]
- Muriel was unhealthily envious of her married friends' family life (object of envy: family life).

    Muriel's unhealthy envy was both ego and non-ego in nature. She held the following attitudes: 'I must have a family like my friends do. Not having what I want in this regard is unbearable [non-ego] and proves that I am unlovable [ego].'
- Phil was unhealthily envious of his friend's promotion (object of envy: achievement).

    Phil's unhealthy envy was largely ego in nature. He held the following rigid/extreme attitudes: 'My friend absolutely should not have got promotion when I didn't. The fact that he did and I didn't proves that I am a rotten person.'
- Mr and Mrs Smith were both unhealthily envious of their friends' lavish lifestyle (object of envy: lifestyle).

    Their unhealthy envy was largely non-ego in nature and was based on the following shared rigid/extreme attitudes: 'Our friends must not have the lifestyle that we don't have and we can't stand it that they do and we don't.'
- Ben was unhealthily envious of his friend's extroversion (object of envy: personal characteristic).

    Ben's unhealthy envy was largely ego in nature. He held the following rigid/extreme attitudes: 'I must be outgoing like my friend. The fact that I am not proves that he is a better person than I am.'
- Jane was unhealthily envious of Beryl's ability to play the piano (object of envy: talent).

    Jane's unhealthy envy was both ego and non-ego in nature. She held the following rigid/extreme attitudes: 'Beryl must not be able to play the piano better than me. I can't bear the fact that I don't have her talent [non-ego] and because I don't this proves that she is worthier than me [ego].'
- Bill was unhealthily envious of his friend's Porsche (object of envy: possession).

    Bill's unhealthy envy was largely non-ego in nature. He held the following rigid/extreme attitudes: 'Bill must not have a Porsche when I don't have one. I can't bear the fact that he has what I don't have.'

Thinking that stems from unhealthy envy-based rigid/extreme attitudes

When a person holds a unhealthy envy-creating rigid/extreme attitude, this will influence the way that they subsequently think.

Before I discuss these ways of thinking, let me stress an important point about unhealthy envy. At the heart of this type of envy is an inability to bear being in a disadvantaged position. Some instances of unhealthy envy are about making things equal. In one such case, the person is content (albeit for a short period) when they get what they covet in the life of others. Here they are not concerned if others have it, as long as they have it. In the other case, if the person doesn't have whatever it is that they covet in the life of others, their object is to deprive these others of what they covet, to spoil it for them or to destroy it. They are content (again albeit for a short period) that these others don't have what they do not have.

Here are some common examples of such subsequent thinking.

Thinking obsessively about how to get what one envies, regardless of its usefulness

When a person is unhealthily envious and they demand that they must get what the other person has that they lack, they will find it easy to become obsessed with whatever it is that they covet but do not have. Furthermore, they will think obsessively about getting it, regardless of its usefulness to them and regardless of the price they may have to pay (financially and psychologically) in order to get it. In other words, such obsessive thinking flows fairly naturally from their unhealthy envy-based rigid/extreme attitudes.

Thinking about depriving the other person of what one envies

If the person's unhealthy envy-based rigid/extreme attitude is centred on others not having what they do not have, they strengthen their conviction in this attitude by thinking about what they can do to deprive the other of what they have that the person covets. They may picture themself taking whatever it is away from the other and will tend to focus on the pleasure they experience by so depriving them. As they do so, they may justify their actions by telling themself that they are righting a wrong. After all, they argue, it is dreadfully unfair if the other person has what they do not have and they are just making an unfair situation fair by depriving the other of what they covet but do not have.

On the other hand, if the person intends to keep whatever it is that they seek to deprive the other of, then they may picture themself keeping it and may justify their actions by showing themself how much they deserve to have whatever it is that they have coveted.

Thinking about spoiling or destroying what one envies so that the other doesn't have it

If the person can't deprive the other person of the object of their unhealthy envy, they can always make things equal in their mind by having thoughts and images of spoiling or destroying what the other has that they covet. Again, as the person fantasises about spoiling or destroying the other's possession, for example, they tend to gain pleasure from doing so, but find a way of justifying their behaviour to themself accordingly (e.g. restoration of fairness).

Thinking obsessively of how to get what one covets and how to deprive others, spoil things for them or destroy what they have

Here the person combines the thinking consequences discussed above. This cocktail is particularly potent in perpetuating their unhealthy envy-related rigid/extreme attitudes.

Thinking denigrating thoughts about the person who has what one envies

One way that the person can make things equal in their mind when they are feeling unhealthy envy is to denigrate in their mind the person who has what they envy. For example, Robert was unhealthily envious of furniture that his friends Lisa and David had. As a result, he told himself either that they were greedy or that they were too ignorant to appreciate what they had. Thinking this way strengthened his conviction in his unhealthy envy-related attitudes and thus increased the probability that he would experience unhealthy envy in the future.

Thinking denigrating thoughts about the object of one's unhealthy envy

A similar equalising mental technique is for the person to denigrate in their mind the object of their unhealthy envy. This is the 'sour grapes' mentality. Thus, if a person covets the grapes that their friend has that they do not have, they can equalise this state of affairs for themself by thinking that the grapes are probably sour. This will help them to feel better momentarily, but in the longer term it will strengthen their conviction in their unhealthy envy-based rigid/extreme attitude and its distorted thinking conclusion: 'I must have what the other person has, and if I can't get it, it's not worth having.'

Trying to convince oneself that one is happy with what one has and that one doesn't really desire what one envies

Another way of making things equal in the person's mind is for them to attempt to convince themself that they are happy with what they have and that they do not really want what they do, in reality, envy. Thus, if the person covets their friend's grapes (and holds unhealthy envy-related rigid/extreme attitudes towards this situation), they will tend to make things equal in their mind by attempting to convince themself that the banana that they have is all that they really want, when it isn't.

They can, of course, combine this strategy with the previous one and attempt to show themself (a) that their banana is all that they really want and (b) that their friend's grapes are, in all probability, sour.

Denying that one feels unhealthily envious

A number of the above thinking strategies involve the person lying to themself. This serves to perpetuate their unhealthy envy-related rigid/extreme attitudes in that first they embellish these attitudes and, second, they are prevented from investigating them, and therefore from changing them, by in effect denying that they feel unhealthy envy in the first place when in truth they do.

A stark and successful example of this is outright denial to themself that they do, in fact, feel unhealthy envy or attempting to convince themself that their envy is really healthy. An example of the former is to tell themself: 'No, I really don't want that' (when they really do), and an example of the latter is to tell themself: 'Yes, I would like that, but I don't need it' (when in reality they do hold the attitude that they do really need it). If the person can delude themself in these ways, this serves to keep their unhealthy envy-based rigid/extreme attitudes alive, making them vulnerable to unhealthy envy even though they will not admit to feeling it.

Behaviour that stems from unhealthy envy-based rigid/extreme attitudes

When a person holds unhealthy envy-based rigid/extreme attitudes, they will tend to act in certain ways. When they do act in these ways, they rehearse and therefore strengthen their conviction in these rigid/extreme attitudes.

Seeking out what one envies whether one really wants it or not

Once the person has identified the object of their unhealthy envy, they tend to devote a great deal of their time and effort to pursuing it whether or not it is healthy for them to do so and whether or not it is really what they want. Such striving will reinforce their unhealthy envy-based rigid/extreme attitudes.

Once one gets what one envies, one puts it to one side and focuses on something else to envy

If the person is successful in getting what they envy, they tend to put it to one side and look around for something else they covet that they don't have. When they find it, they once again tend to pursue it in a very single-minded manner, while rehearsing their unhealthy envy-based rigid/extreme attitudes. They continue this pattern until it becomes second nature to them.

When they put aside the object that they envied and obtained (after much striving), they reinforce the idea that what is essential to them is to get rid of the deprivation of not having what they think they must have rather than enjoying the envied object itself.

Other behaviour that stems from unhealthy envy-based rigid/extreme attitudes

The following behaviours involve the person putting into practice the thinking strategies discussed above. Thus, the person:

- Actively attempts to take away what they envy from the other.
- Actively attempts to spoil or destroy the envied object.

- Verbally disparages the person who has what they envy.
- Verbally disparages the envied object to others.
- Tells others that they don't really want what they envy.

It is important to appreciate that the person will rehearse their specific unhealthy envy-based rigid/extreme attitudes while carrying out these behaviours.

People develop and rehearse general unhealthy envy-based rigid/extreme attitudes

General unhealthy envy-based rigid/extreme attitudes are attitudes that the person holds in many theme-related situations that lead them to experience unhealthy envy in these situations. If they develop and rehearse such attitudes, they will experience unhealthy envy in many different situations. They will do this mainly because they will become prone to focus on what they covet in the life of others that they don't have. Once the person demands that they must have what they covet in the life of others, they will focus on what they don't have and edit out what they do have. Having identified a specific envy object in this way, they bring to it a specific variant of their general unhealthy envy-based rigid/extreme attitude so that they make themself unhealthily envious in this situation.

Having made themself feel unhealthily envious in this way, the person then tends to think and act in ways that are consistent with their unhealthy envy-based rigid/extreme attitudes and doing so strengthens their conviction in these attitudes. This increases the chance that they will perpetuate their unhealthy envy.

People develop and rehearse a view of the world founded on unhealthy envy-based rigid/extreme attitudes

For the last time, I want to stress that people develop world views that render them vulnerable to particular unhealthy negative emotions. The world views that render a person vulnerable to unhealthy envy do so because they make it very easy for them to focus on what they don't have (and covet) and to edit out in their mind what they do have. Then, as I have shown earlier in the chapter, the person makes themself unhealthily envious about this situation with the appropriate rigid/extreme attitudes. Here is an illustrative list of unhealthy envy-related world views that the person tends to develop and rehearse, and the inferences that they spawn.

World view: The grass is always greener in the lives of others.
Inference: Whatever I have is less attractive than what others have.

World view: Satisfaction can be achieved only if I get what I want.
Inference: If I get what I covet, it will satisfy me. [This, of course, is a delusion, since unhealthy envy-related rigid/extreme attitudes render the person insatiable.]

World view: It's unfair if others have what I don't have, but it is fair if I have what others don't have.
Inference: If I don't have something that I covet that someone else has, this inequality is unfair.

World view: People's worth is defined by what they have in life.
Inference: People will like me for what I have, rather than for who I am.

World view: The more I have, the happier I'll be.
Inference: In any situation, it is better to have what I don't have than to be content with what I do have.

In the final chapter, I will discuss healthy envy, which is the healthy alternative to unhealthy envy.

Further reading

Academic

Salovey, P. (Ed.) (1991). *The psychology of jealousy and envy.* New York: Guilford.

Self-help

Dryden, W. (2010). *Coping with envy.* London: Sheldon Press.

Chapter 16

Understanding healthy envy

As with other healthy negative emotions, the components of healthy envy are clear, but what to call it is more difficult. I will use the term 'healthy envy' in this chapter as I have previously referred to the healthy types of anger and jealousy as 'healthy anger' and 'healthy jealousy' respectively. However, you will find others referring to 'healthy envy', 'non-malicious envy' and even 'admiring envy'. The important thing to recognise, of course, is that we are discussing a healthy alternative to unhealthy envy.

The components of healthy envy

When a person experiences healthy envy:

1 They make certain types of inference.
2 They bring a set of healthy envy-based flexible/non-extreme attitudes to those inferences.
3 They think in ways that are consistent with the above flexible/non-extreme attitudes.
4 They act in ways that are consistent with these flexible/non-extreme attitudes.
5 They rehearse a general version of their specific healthy envy-based flexible/non-extreme attitudes which helps them to see the world more objectively than when they utilise and rehearse general unhealthy envy-based rigid and extreme attitudes.
6 They develop and rehearse a healthy envy-based world view.

Now let me deal with these issues one at a time.

Inference in healthy envy

When a person experiences healthy envy as a healthy alternative to unhealthy envy, they make the same inference as they do when they experience unhealthy envy. Again, this inference does not have to reflect accurately what is happening or what has happened. The important point is that the person thinks that it is true. The main inference in healthy envy is as follows: *someone has someone or something in their life that the person does not have in their own life, but which they prize and desire.*

The person holds and rehearses flexible/non-extreme attitudes towards the inference

Once again, I want to stress that a person's healthy envy is not caused by their inference that another person has something (or someone) that they want but do not have. Rather, these healthy feelings are largely determined by the flexible/non-extreme attitudes that the person holds towards this inference, true or not.

As with unhealthy envy, there are two different types of healthy envy: healthy ego envy and healthy non-ego envy, although a person may have both.

Healthy ego envy

In healthy ego envy the person does not invest their self-esteem in whatever it is that others have that they want but don't have. When the person experiences healthy envy in the ego domain, they hold one flexible attitude and one non-extreme attitude:

- A flexible attitude (e.g. 'A colleague got promoted and I wish that I had got promoted as well, but this did not have to happen').
- A non-extreme unconditional self-acceptance attitude (e.g. 'I am not less worthy than my colleague for not getting promoted. We are both equal in human worth just because we are alive, but we are unequal in the fact that they got promoted and I didn't.').

Healthy non-ego envy

In healthy non-ego envy, the person is unhappy but not disturbed about not having what they want. Here they are focused on their sense of non-ego deprivation. When the person experiences healthy envy in the non-ego domain, they hold one flexible attitude and one non-extreme attitude:

- A flexible attitude (e.g. 'A colleague got promoted and I wish that I had got promoted as well, but this did not have to happen').
- A non-extreme bearability attitude (e.g. 'It is difficult for me to bear the situation where my colleague got promoted and I didn't. However, I can bear it, it is worth it to me to do so, I am willing to bear it and I am going to do so.').

The role of flexible/non-extreme attitudes in healthy envy: The examples revisited (see Chapter 15)

In Chapter 15, I discussed a number of examples of unhealthy envy. Let me now return to these examples and show which attitudes the person would have to hold in order to experience healthy envy instead.

- In order for Barry to experience healthy non-ego envy of his friend's attractive wife, he would have to hold the following flexible/non-extreme attitudes: 'I would like to have an attractive wife like my friend has, but I don't have to have one. I don't like not having one, but I can bear this situation and it's worth it to me to do so. Furthermore, I am willing to bear this situation and I am going to do so.'
- In order for Linda to experience healthy ego envy of her friend's good looks, she would have to hold the following flexible/non-extreme attitudes: 'I would like to be as attractive as my friend, but I don't have to be. I am not less worthy than her because I am less attractive than her. We are equal in worth but unequal in physical attractiveness.'
- In order for Muriel to experience healthy ego and non-ego envy of her married friends' family life, she would have to hold the following flexible/non-extreme attitudes: 'I would very much like to have a family like my friends do, but this is not necessary for me. Not having what I want in this regard is bearable [non-ego] and does not prove that I am unlovable. I am the same lovable person with or without a family like my friends [ego].'

Understanding healthy envy 215

- In order for Phil to experience healthy ego envy of his friend's promotion, he would have to hold the following flexible/non-extreme attitudes: 'I would prefer it if my friend hadn't got promoted when I didn't, but my preference does not have to be met. The fact that he did and I didn't does not prove that I am a rotten person. I am an ordinary, fallible human being whose worth does not vary.'
- In order for Mr and Mrs Smith to experience healthy non-ego envy of their friends' lavish lifestyle, they would have to hold the following flexible/non-extreme attitudes: 'We would prefer it if our friends did not have the lifestyle that we don't have, but it does not follow that they must not have such a lifestyle. It's hard to bear it if they do and we don't, but it is bearable and worth bearing. We are willing to bear this situation and we are going to do so.'
- In order for Ben to experience healthy ego envy of his friend's extroversion, he would have to hold the following flexible/non-extreme attitudes: 'I would like to be outgoing like my friend, but I don't have to be. The fact that I am not does not prove that he is a better person than I am. We are both equal as persons even if we are unequal in extroversion.'
- In order for Jane to experience healthy ego and non-ego envy of Beryl's ability to play the piano, she would have to hold the following flexible/non-extreme attitudes: 'I don't want Beryl to be able to play the piano better than me, but it does not have to be the way I want it. I can bear the fact that I don't have her talent [non-ego] and it does not prove that she is worthier than me. We are equal in worth [ego].'
- In order for Bill to experience healthy non-ego envy of his friend's Porsche, he would have to hold the following flexible/non-extreme attitudes: 'I would prefer it if Bill did not have a Porsche when I don't have one. However, I can bear the fact that he has what I don't have. It's worth bearing, I'm willing to do so and I am going to do so.'

Thinking that stems from healthy envy-based flexible/non-extreme attitudes

When a person holds a healthy envy-related flexible/non-extreme attitude, this will influence the way that they subsequently think.

Here are some common examples of such subsequent thinking.

Thinking non-obsessively about how to get what one envies only if it is useful to the person

When a person holds healthy envy-based attitudes, they will not become obsessed with whatever it is that they covet but do not have. Given this, they will be able to stand back and think clearly about the usefulness of the object in the context of the price they may have to pay (financially and psychologically) in order to get it. They will only think about how to get the object if it is truly useful to the person and the price of doing so is worth it to the person.

Allowing the other person to have and enjoy the desired possession without denigrating that person or the possession

When a person holds healthy envy-based attitudes, they are not threatened by another person having something that they covet but lack. Consequently they do not think about depriving the person of what they have, nor do they denigrate the possession or the person who has it. Also they do not think about spoiling or destroying the object so that the other does not have it.

Being honest with oneself if one is not happy with one's possessions, rather than defensively trying to convince oneself that one is happy with them when one is not

When a person experiences unhealthy envy, they try to make things equal in their mind and, as we saw in the last chapter, one way a person tries to do this is to attempt to convince themself that they are happy with what they have and that they do not really want what they do, in reality, envy. However, when the person holds healthy envy-based attitudes, they don't have this 'making things equal' mentality. Consequently, they can be honest with themself and acknowledge in their mind that they are not happy with their possessions when this is the case.

Acknowledging that they do feel healthily envious

When a person holds healthy envy-based attitudes, they can admit to themself that they are feeling envy and would like what they lack but another has. As they are not threatened by things not being equal (although they do not like this), they do not have to lie to themself.

Behaviour that stems from healthy envy-based flexible/non-extreme attitudes

When a person holds healthy envy-based flexible/non-extreme attitudes, they will tend to act in certain ways.

Admitting to others that one does feel healthily envious

When a person holds healthy envy-based attitudes, they are not threatened by their feelings of healthy envy, and not only are they able to admit to themself that they feel envious, but they are also able to admit this to others.[1]

Seeking out what one envies only when one really wants it and the cost of doing so is worth it

As I showed above, when a person holds healthy envy-based attitudes, they are able to think non-obsessively about the desired object and think how to get it only if they really want it, it is useful to them and the cost of getting it is worth accepting. If the person has decided that they are going to seek out what they envy, then they implement doing so without neglecting their other responsibilities.

People develop and rehearse general healthy envy-based flexible/non-extreme attitudes

General healthy envy-based flexible/non-extreme attitudes are attitudes that a person holds in many theme-related situations that enable them to experience healthy envy in these situations. Developing and rehearsing such attitudes will enable the person to experience healthy envy in many different situations, but only when they really want what the other has and they lack but covet and they can make use of it, or when they can admire what the other has that they don't have but would like to have.

People develop and rehearse a view of the world founded on healthy envy-based flexible/non-extreme attitudes

For the final time, let me stress that people develop world views that render them vulnerable to or protect them from particular unhealthy negative emotions. The world views that underpin a person's tendency to experience healthy envy rather than unhealthy envy are as follows, together with the inferences that they spawn.

World view: The grass may seem greener in the lives of others, but this is often not the case at closer inspection.
Inference: Some of what I have is less attractive than what others have, but in other cases it is just as attractive or even more attractive.

World view: Satisfaction can be achieved in a number of ways and not only if I get what I want.
Inference: If I get what I covet, it will satisfy me if I truly want it, but I can achieve satisfaction in other ways.

World view: If others have what I don't have, that may be unfair, but from a different perspective it may be fair. Also if I have what others don't have, that may be fair or again, from a different perspective, it may be unfair.
Inference: If I don't have something that I covet that someone else has, this inequality may be unfair, but not necessarily.

World view: People's worth is defined by their aliveness, fallibility and being human rather than by what they have in life.
Inference: Some people will like me for what I have, but others will like me for who I am.

World view: Happiness depends more on one's attitudes than on one's possessions.
Inference: I can be content with what I do have in life, but I can still seek out what I covet if it will improve the quality of my life in the longer term.

We have now come to the end of this book. I have provided a summary of the points made in abbreviated form in the Appendix, which can serve as an aide-mémoire when one needs such information in capsule form. I welcome feedback to windy@windydryden.com

Note

1 It is, of course, much more difficult for the person to admit to others that they experience problematic envy, given its much darker side, as shown in the previous chapter.

Appendix

List of eight common unhealthy negative emotions with the equivalent healthy negative emotions, together with their adversity themes, basic attitudes, behaviours and forms of subsequent thinking

Anxiety vs concern

Adversity	• You are facing a threat to your personal domain	
Basic Attitude	**RIGID AND EXTREME**	**FLEXIBLE AND NON-EXTREME**
Emotion	Anxiety	Concern
Behaviour	• You avoid the threat • You withdraw physically from the threat • You ward off the threat (e.g. by rituals or superstitious behaviour) • You try to neutralise the threat (e.g. by being nice to people of whom you are afraid) • You distract yourself from the threat by engaging in other activity • You keep checking on the current status of the threat, hoping to find that it has disappeared or become benign • You seek reassurance from others that the threat is benign • You seek support from others so that if the threat happens, they will handle it or be there to rescue you • You overprepare in order to minimise the threat happening or so that you are prepared to meet it (NB it is the overpreparation that is the problem here) • You tranquillise your feelings so that you don't think about the threat • You overcompensate for feeling vulnerable by seeking out an even greater threat to prove to yourself that you can cope	• You face up to the threat without using any safety-seeking measures • You take constructive action to deal with the threat • You seek support from others to help you face up to the threat and then take constructive action by yourself rather than rely on them to handle it for you or to be there to rescue you • You prepare to meet the threat but do not overprepare

Subsequent Thinking	Threat-exaggerated thinking	
	• You overestimate the probability of the threat occurring • You underestimate your ability to cope with the threat • You ruminate about the threat • You create an even more negative threat in your mind • You magnify the negative consequences of the threat and minimise its positive consequences • You have more task-irrelevant thoughts than in the case of concern	• You are realistic about the probability of the threat occurring • You view the threat realistically • You realistically appraise your ability to cope with the threat • You think about what to do concerning dealing with the threat constructively rather than ruminate about the threat • You have more task-relevant thoughts than in the case of anxiety • You picture yourself dealing with the threat in a realistic way
	Safety-seeking thinking	
	• You withdraw mentally from the threat • You try to persuade yourself that the threat is not imminent and that you are 'imagining' it • You think in ways designed to reassure yourself that the threat is benign or, if not, that its consequences will be insignificant • You distract yourself from the threat, e.g. by focusing on mental scenes of safety and well-being • You overprepare mentally in order to minimise the threat happening or so that you are prepared to meet it (NB once again it is the overpreparation that is the problem here) • You picture yourself dealing with the threat in a masterful way • You overcompensate for your feeling of vulnerability by picturing yourself dealing effectively with an even bigger threat	

Depression[1] vs sadness

Adversity	• You have experienced a loss from the sociotropic and/or autonomous realms of your personal domain • You have experienced failure within the sociotropic and/or autonomous realms of your personal domain • You or others have experienced an undeserved plight	
Basic Attitude	**RIGID AND EXTREME**	**FLEXIBLE AND NON-EXTREME**
Emotion	Depression	Sadness
Behaviour	• You become overly dependent on and seek to cling to others (particularly in sociotropic depression) • You bemoan your fate or that of others to anyone who will listen (particularly in pity-based depression) • You create an environment consistent with your depressed feelings • You attempt to terminate feelings of depression in self-destructive ways • You either push away attempts to comfort you (in autonomous depression) or use such comfort to reinforce your dependency (in sociotropic depression) or your self- or other-pity (in pity-based depression)	• You seek out reinforcements after a period of mourning (particularly when your inferential theme is loss) • You create an environment inconsistent with depressed feelings • You express your feelings about the loss, failure or undeserved plight and talk in a non-complaining way about these feelings to significant others • You allow yourself to be comforted in a way that helps you to express your feelings of sadness and mourn your loss
Subsequent Thinking	• You see only negative aspects of the loss, failure or undeserved plight • You think of other losses, failures and undeserved plights that you (and, in the case of the latter, others) have experienced • You think you are unable to help yourself (helplessness) • You only see pain and blackness in the future (hopelessness) • You see yourself being totally dependent on others (in autonomous depression) • You see yourself as being disconnected from others (in sociotropic depression) • You see the world as full of undeservedness and unfairness (in plight-based depression) • You tend to ruminate concerning the source of your depression and its consequences	• You are able to recognise both negative and positive aspects of the loss or failure • You think you are able to help yourself • You look to the future with hope

1 Here I will refer to depression that is non-clinical in nature.

Shame vs disappointment

Adversity	• Something highly negative has been revealed about you (or about a group with whom you identify) by yourself or by others • You have acted in a way that falls very short of your ideal • Others look down on or shun you (or a group with whom you identify) or you think that they do	
Basic Attitude	RIGID AND EXTREME	FLEXIBLE AND NON-EXTREME
Emotion	Shame	Disappointment
Behaviour	• You remove yourself from the 'gaze' of others • You isolate yourself from others • You save face by attacking other(s) who have 'shamed' you • You defend your threatened self-esteem in self-defeating ways • You ignore attempts by others to restore social equilibrium	• You continue to participate actively in social interaction • You respond positively to attempts of others to restore social equilibrium
Subsequent Thinking	• You overestimate the negativity of the information revealed • You overestimate the likelihood that the judging group will notice or be interested in the information • You overestimate the degree of disapproval you (or your reference group) will receive • You overestimate how long any disapproval will last	• You see the information revealed in a compassionate self-accepting context • You are realistic about the likelihood that the judging group will notice or be interested in the information revealed • You are realistic about the degree of disapproval youyou're your reference group) will receive • You are realistic about how long any disapproval will last

Guilt vs remorse

Adversity	• You have broken your moral code • You have failed to live up to your moral code • You have hurt someone's feelings	
Basic Attitude	RIGID AND EXTREME	FLEXIBLE AND NON-EXTREME
Emotion	Guilt	Remorse
Behaviour	• You escape from the unhealthy pain of guilt in self-defeating ways • You beg forgiveness from the person you have wronged • You promise unrealistically that you will not 'sin' again • You punish yourself physically or by deprivation • You defensively disclaim responsibility for wrongdoing • You make excuses for your behaviour • You reject offers of forgiveness	• You face up to the healthy pain that accompanies the realisation that you have sinned • You ask, but do not beg, for forgiveness • You understand the reasons for your wrongdoing and act on your understanding • You atone for the sin by taking a penalty • You make appropriate amends • You do not make excuses for your behaviour or enact other defensive behaviour • You accept offers for forgiveness
Subsequent Thinking	• You conclude that you have definitely committed the sin • You assume more personal responsibility than the situation warrants • You assign far less responsibility to others than is warranted • You dismiss possible mitigating factors for your behaviour • You only see your behaviour in a guilt-related context and fail to put it into an overall context • You think that you will receive retribution	• You take into account all relevant data when judging whether or not you have 'sinned' • You assume an appropriate level of personal responsibility • You assign an appropriate level of responsibility to others • You take into account mitigating factors • You put your behaviour into overall context • You think you may be penalised rather than receive retribution

Unhealthy anger vs healthy anger

Adversity	You think that you have been frustrated in some way or your movement towards an important goal has been obstructed in some way • Someone has treated you badly • Someone has transgressed one of your personal rules • You have transgressed one of your own personal rules • Someone or something has threatened your self-esteem or disrespected you	
Basic Attitude	**RIGID AND EXTREME**	**FLEXIBLE AND NON-EXTREME**
Emotion	Unhealthy anger	Healthy anger
Behaviour	• You attack the other(s) physically • You attack the other(s) verbally • You attack the other(s) passive-aggressively • You displace the attack on to another person, animal or object • You withdraw aggressively • You recruit allies against the other(s)	• You assert yourself with the other(s) • You request, but do not demand, behavioural change from the other(s) • You leave an unsatisfactory situation non-aggressively after taking steps to deal with it
Subsequent Thinking	• You overestimate the extent to which the other(s) acted deliberately • You see malicious intent in the motives of the other(s) • You see yourself as definitely right and the other(s) as definitely wrong • You are unable to see the point of view of the other(s) • You plot to exact revenge • You ruminate about the other's behaviour and imagine coming out on top	• You think that the other(s) may have acted deliberately, but you also recognise that this may not have been the case • You are able to see the point of view of the other(s) • You have fleeting, rather than sustained, thoughts to exact revenge • You think that other(s) may have had malicious intent in their motives, but you also recognise that this may not have been the case • You think that you are probably rather than definitely right and the other(s) is probably rather than definitely wrong

Hurt vs sorrow

Adversity	• Others treat you badly (and you think you do not deserve such treatment) • You think that the other person is less invested in your relationship than you are	
Basic Attitude	**RIGID AND EXTREME**	**FLEXIBLE AND NON-EXTREME**
Emotion	Hurt	Sorrow
Behaviour	• You stop communicating with the other person • You sulk and make obvious you feel hurt without disclosing details of the matter • You indirectly criticise or punish the other person for their offence • You tell others how badly you have been treated, but don't take any responsibility for any contribution you may have made to this	• You communicate your feelings to the other directly • You request that the other person acts in a fairer manner towards you • You discuss the situation with others in a balanced way, focusing on the way you have been treated and taking responsibility for any contribution you may have made to this
Subsequent Thinking	• You overestimate the unfairness of the other person's behaviour • You think that the other person does not care for you or is indifferent to you • You see yourself as alone, uncared for or misunderstood • You tend to think of past 'hurts' • You think that the other person has to make the first move to you and you dismiss the possibility of making the first move towards that person	• You are realistic about the degree of unfairness in the other person's behaviour • You think that the other person has acted badly rather than as demonstrating lack of caring or indifference • You see yourself as being in a poor situation, but still connected to, cared for by and understood by others not directly involved in the situation • If you think of past 'hurts', you do so with less frequency and less intensity than when you now feel hurt • You are open to the idea of making the first move towards the other person

Unhealthy jealousy vs healthy jealousy
(concern for your relationship)

Adversity	• A threat is posed to your relationship with your partner by a third person • A threat is posed by uncertainty you face concerning your partner's whereabouts, behaviour or thinking in the context of the first threat	
Basic Attitude	RIGID AND EXTREME	FLEXIBLE AND NON-EXTREME
Emotion	Unhealthy jealousy	Healthy jealousy (concern for your relationship)
Behaviour	• You seek constant reassurance that you are loved • You monitor the actions and feelings of your partner • You search for evidence that your partner is involved with someone else • You attempt to restrict the movements or activities of your partner • You set tests which your partner has to pass • You retaliate for your partner's presumed infidelity • You sulk	• You allow your partner to initiate expressing love for you without prompting them or seeking reassurance once they have done so • You allow your partner freedom without monitoring their feelings, actions and whereabouts • You allow your partner to show natural interest in members of the opposite sex without setting tests • You communicate your concern for your relationship in an open and non-blaming manner
Subsequent Thinking	• You exaggerate any threat to your relationship that does exist • You think the loss of your relationship is imminent • You misconstrue your partner's ordinary conversations with relevant others as having romantic or sexual connotations • You construct visual images of your partner's infidelity • If your partner admits to finding another person attractive, you think that they find that person more attractive than you and that they will leave you for this other person	• You tend not to exaggerate any threat to your relationship that does exist • You do not misconstrue ordinary conversations between your partner and other men/women • You do not construct visual images of your partner's infidelity • You accept that your partner will find others attractive but you do not see this as a threat

Unhealthy envy vs healthy envy

Adversity	Another person possesses and enjoys something desirable that you do not have	
Basic Attitude	**RIGID AND EXTREME**	**FLEXIBLE AND NON-EXTREME**
Emotion	Unhealthy envy	Healthy envy
Behaviour	• You disparage verbally to others the person who has the desired possession • You disparage verbally to others the desired possession • If you had the chance, you would take away the desired possession from the other (either so that you will have it or so that the other is deprived of it) • If you had the chance, you would spoil or destroy the desired possession so that the other person does not have it	• You admit to others that you feel healthily envious • You strive to obtain the desired possession if it is truly what you want
Subsequent Thinking	• You tend to denigrate in your mind the value of the desired possession and/or the person who possesses it • You try to convince yourself that you are happy with your possessions (although you are not) • You think about how to acquire the desired possession regardless of its usefulness • You think about how to deprive the other person of the desired possession • You think about how to spoil or destroy the other's desired possession • You think about all the other things the other has that you don't have	• You honestly admit to yourself that you covet the desired possession • You are honest with yourself if you are not happy with your possessions, rather than defensively trying to convince yourself that you are happy with them when you are not • You think about how to obtain the desired possession because you desire it for healthy reasons • You can allow the other person to have and enjoy the desired possession without denigrating that person or the possession • You think about what the other has and lacks and what you have and lack

Index

aggressive withdrawal 141
anger *see* healthy anger; unhealthy anger
anxiety 3, 220–1; behavioural consequences 9–10; general anxiety-creating philosophy (GAP) 4–8; health 15–17; inferences 8, 17–20; losing self-control 13–14; meta-disturbance 12–13; panic attacks 18–19; social 17–18; thinking consequences 10–12; threat 3–4, 7–8; uncertainty 14–15; world views 19–20; *see also* concern
appreciation 160
attitudes *see* flexible/non-extreme attitudes; rigid/extreme attitudes
autonomous depression 44–51
autonomous loss 46–8, 63–4
autonomous sadness 61–4
awfulising attitude: anxiety 5–6; depression 40–1; hurt 162

bearability attitude: concern 23–4; healthy envy 214; healthy jealousy 192–3; sadness 59–60, 63; sorrow 170
Beck, A.T. 3
begging forgiveness 112
behavioural consequences: anxiety 9–10; concern 27–8; depression 42, 46–7, 55; disappointment 96–7; guilt 111–15; healthy anger 151–2; healthy envy 217; healthy jealousy 194–6; hurt 164–5; remorse 123–5; sadness 60, 63–4, 67–8; shame 83–5; sorrow 172; unhealthy anger 138–41; unhealthy envy 209–10; unhealthy jealousy 183–8
betrayal 159

cathartic anger 140–1
concern 21, 220–1; behavioural consequences 27–8; bodily symptoms of anxiety 33–4; general concern-related philosophy (GCP) 22–6; health 31–2; losing self-control 29–30; social 32–3; thinking consequences 28; threat 21, 25–6; uncertainty 30–1; world views and inferences 34–5; *see also* anxiety
confession 111–12
consequences *see* behavioural consequences; thinking consequences
criticism 158

depression 39, 222; autonomous depression 44–51; behavioural consequences 42, 46–7, 55; deepening 49–51; meta-disturbance 54–5; metaphors and images 44, 49; other-pity 53–4; physical aspects 54–6,

67; self-acceptance 68–9; self-devaluation 40, 45–6, 55; self-pity 51–3; sociotropic 39–44, 49–51; thinking consequences 42–4, 47–9, 55; world views and inferences 47–8, 51–4, 56; *see also* sadness
devaluation attitude *see* other-devaluation attitude; self-devaluation attitude
disappointment 89, 223; attitude towards self 93; behavioural consequences 96–7; external events 93–4; general flexible/non-extreme attitudes 97–8; inferences 90, 98; root flexible/non-extreme attitudes 90–3; thinking consequences 94–6; world views 98; *see also* shame
disapproval 159
disrespect 136, 149–50

envy *see* healthy envy; unhealthy envy
exaggeration 108–9
exclusion 160
extreme attitudes *see* rigid/extreme attitudes

flexible preference: concern 22–3; disappointment 90–4; healthy anger 146–7; healthy envy 213–14; healthy jealousy 192–4; remorse 119–21; sadness 59, 61–2; sorrow 170
flexible/non-extreme attitudes: concern 22–8, 34–5; disappointment 90–8; healthy anger 145–52; healthy envy 213–18; healthy jealousy 192–7; remorse 119–25; sadness 64–9; sadness (autonomous) 61–4; sadness (sociotropic) 58–61; sorrow 169–73; *see also* bearability attitude; non-awfulising attitude; unconditional self-acceptance attitude
frustration 134–5, 147–8

general anxiety-creating philosophy (GAP) 4–8

general concern-related philosophy (GCP) 22–5
guilt 101–2, 224; behavioural consequences 111–15; general rigid/extreme attitudes 115–16; inferences 102–3, 116–17; negative self-judgements 104–7; root rigid/extreme attitudes 103–4; thinking consequences 108–11; unconditional 107–8; world views 116–17; *see also* remorse

health anxiety 15–17
health concern 31–2
healthy anger 144–5, 225; behavioural consequences 151–2; ego and non-ego anger 145–7; general flexible/non-extreme attitudes 152; inferences 145, 152–3; root flexible/non-extreme attitudes 145–50; thinking consequences 150–1; world views 152–3; *see also* unhealthy anger
healthy envy 212, 228; behavioural consequences 217; ego and non-ego 213–15; general flexible/non-extreme attitudes 217; inferences 213, 217–18; root flexible/non-extreme attitudes 213–15; thinking consequences 215–16; world views 217–18; *see also* unhealthy envy
healthy jealousy 191, 227; behavioural consequences 194–6; general flexible/non-extreme attitudes 196; inferences 192, 196–7; root flexible/non-extreme attitudes 192–4; thinking consequences 194; world views 196–7; *see also* unhealthy jealousy
healthy negative emotions *see* concern; disappointment; healthy anger; healthy envy; healthy jealousy; remorse; sadness; sorrow
hindsight 110
hurt 157, 226; behavioural consequences 164–5; ego and

Index

non-ego hurt 161–2; general rigid/extreme attitudes 165–6; inferences 157–60, 167; root rigid/extreme attitudes 161–2; thinking consequences 162–4; world views 167; *see also* sorrow

if only thinking 109–10
inferences: anxiety 8, 17–20; concern 34–5; depression 47–8, 51–4, 56; disappointment 90, 98; guilt 102–3, 116–17; healthy anger 145, 152–3; healthy envy 213, 217–18; healthy jealousy 192, 196–7; hurt 157–60, 167; remorse 119, 125; sadness 69; shame 74–6, 87; sorrow 168–9, 173–4; unhealthy anger 130–1, 142–3; unhealthy envy 202–3, 210–11; unhealthy jealousy 178–9, 189
injustice/unfairness 135, 148–9
irrational beliefs *see* rigid/extreme attitudes

jealousy *see* healthy jealousy; unhealthy jealousy

loss *see* depression; sadness

meta-disturbance: anxiety 12–13; depression 54–5

negative self-judgement *see* self-devaluation attitude
neglect 159–60
non-awfulising attitude: concern 23; sorrow 170
non-extreme attitudes *see* flexible/non-extreme attitudes

other-devaluation attitude 133–5, 162
other-pity 53–4, 66–7

panic attacks 18–19, 33–4
partners *see* healthy jealousy; unhealthy jealousy
passive-aggressive behaviour 139–40
penance 113

pity *see* other-pity; plight pity; self-pity

rational beliefs *see* flexible/non-extreme attitudes
reassurance seeking 114–15
rejection 158
relationships *see* healthy jealousy; unhealthy jealousy
remorse 118, 224; behavioural consequences 123–5; general flexible/non-extreme attitudes 125; inferences 119, 125; root flexible/non-extreme attitudes 119–21; thinking consequences 122–3; world views 125; *see also* guilt
responsibility 84–5, 97, 109, 113–14
revenge 139
revenge fantasy 137–8
rigid demand: anxiety 4–5; depression 40, 44–5; guilt 103–4; hurt 161–2; shame 77–8; unhealthy anger 133–6; unhealthy envy 203–5; unhealthy jealousy 180–1
rigid/extreme attitudes: anxiety 4–7, 9–16, 19; depression 51–6; depression (autonomous) 44–51; depression (sociotropic) 39–44, 50–1; guilt 103–16; hurt 161–7; shame 76–87; unhealthy anger 132–42; unhealthy envy 203–11; unhealthy jealousy 179–89; *see also* rigid attitude; self-devaluation attitude; unbearability attitude

sadness 58, 69–70, 222; about depression 67–9; autonomous 61–4; behavioural consequences 60, 63–4, 67–8; metaphors and images 61, 64; plight pity 64–7; sociotropic 58–61; thinking consequences 61, 64, 67; world views and inferences 69; *see also* depression
safety-seeking thinking 11–12
self-control anxiety 13–14

Index

self-control concern 29–30
self-devaluation attitude: anxiety 6–7; depression 40, 45–6, 55; guilt 103–7; hurt 161–2; shame 77–80; unhealthy anger 133–6; unhealthy envy 203; unhealthy jealousy 180–1
self-esteem threat 135, 149
self-pity 51–3, 64–6
selfishness 106–7
shame 73, 223; behavioural consequences 83–5; external causes 80; general rigid/extreme attitudes 85–7; inferences 74–6, 87; negative self-judgements 78–80; root rigid/extreme attitudes 76–8; thinking consequences 81–3; unconditional 81; world views 87; *see also* disappointment
sinning *see* guilt
social anxiety 17–18
social concern 32–3
sociotropic depression 39–44, 49–51
sociotropic loss 41–3, 60–1
sociotropic sadness 58–61
sorrow 168, 226; behavioural consequences 172; ego and non-ego 169–70; general flexible/non-extreme attitudes 173; inferences 168–9, 173–4; root flexible/non-extreme attitudes 169–70; thinking consequences 170–2; world views 173–4; *see also* hurt
subsequent thinking *see* thinking consequences
sulking 164–5

thinking consequences: anxiety 10–12; concern 28; depression 42–4, 47–9, 55; disappointment 94–6; guilt 108–11; healthy anger 150–1; healthy envy 215–16; healthy jealousy 194; hurt 162–4; remorse 122–3; sadness 61, 64, 67; shame 81–3; sorrow 170–2; unhealthy anger 136–8; unhealthy envy 206–9; unhealthy jealousy 181–3

threat 3–4, 7–8, 21
threat-exaggerated thinking 10–12
transgression 133–4, 147

unbearability attitude: anxiety 6; depression 40–1; hurt 162; unhealthy envy 204
uncertainty anxiety 14–15
uncertainty concern 30–1
unconditional guilt 107–8
unconditional self-acceptance attitude: concern 24–5; depression 68–9; disappointment 90–3; healthy envy 213; healthy jealousy 193; remorse 119–21; sadness 59, 62, 68–9; sorrow 170
unconditional shame 81
unhealthy anger 129–30, 225; behavioural consequences 138–41; ego and non-ego 132–3; general rigid/extreme attitudes 141–2; inferences 130–1, 142–3; root rigid/extreme attitudes 132–6; thinking consequences 136–8; world views 142–3; *see also* healthy anger
unhealthy envy 201–2, 228; behavioural consequences 209–10; ego and non-ego 203–5; general rigid/extreme attitudes 210; inferences 202–3, 210–11; root rigid/extreme attitudes 203–5; thinking consequences 206–9; world views 210–11; *see also* healthy envy
unhealthy jealousy 177–8, 227; behavioural consequences 183–8; core rigid/extreme attitudes 179–81; general rigid/extreme attitudes 188–9; inferences 178–9, 189; thinking consequences 181–3; world views 189; *see also* healthy jealousy
unhealthy negative emotions *see* anxiety; depression; guilt; hurt; shame; unhealthy anger; unhealthy envy; unhealthy jealousy

verbal attack 139

Printed in the United States
by Baker & Taylor Publisher Services